James Anson Farrer

Paganism and Christianity

James Anson Farrer

Paganism and Christianity

ISBN/EAN: 9783743382855

Manufactured in Europe, USA, Canada, Australia, Japa

Cover: Foto ©Lupo / pixelio.de

Manufactured and distributed by brebook publishing software (www.brebook.com)

James Anson Farrer

Paganism and Christianity

PAGANISM & CHRISTIANITY

INTRODUCTION

IF any great classical writers of the ancient world, like Seneca or Cicero, could come to life again, nothing surely would astonish them more than the descriptions they might read in our books of the state of the world when they left it, of its moral depravity, and the absence of all religious ideas. One would gladly hear what they would say to it all; but, failing that, it only remains to enter as much as possible into their tone of thought, and to present the case between Christianity and Paganism as they might do if they could now speak for themselves, and had at their command eighteen centuries of Church history and all the writings of the Fathers and theologians.

In assuming on their behalf and in their stead this advocacy of a literature and philosophy, representing a civilisation to which we still owe the main and better elements of our own, I have simply endeavoured to put the case of pre-Christian Paganism in its best and truest light, and to meet and controvert a legion of writers from the time of

Eusebius to our own, who, in the zeal of their piety, have been wont to misrepresent the state of the older world, by the simple process of adding black to its places of darkest shadow, and of noticing in historical Christianity none but the regions of its higher lights. The task of correcting this view involves no reference whatever to Christianity as a religion; its sole concern is with such aspects of the history and teaching of the Church as touched, and therefore can be compared with, earlier systems of theology and ethics. For the claims of truth and justice must be paramount even here, though the matter only regards a long extinct philosophy and a system of belief or fancy whose sole remaining friends are among the poets. It must no longer suffice to conduct to a triumphant issue the comparison between Paganism and Christianity to contrast the worst practices or superstitions of the lower Pagans, not with the practices or superstitions of the Christians at all, but with the highest and unapproached ideals of the foremost Christian teachers; to be fair we must compare ideals with ideals, the best teaching of the one with the best teaching of the other, the Philosophers with the Fathers, in order to arrive at results which may correspond with real truth, not merely with foregone conclusions.

The fashion alluded to, of conveying a false impression of classical literature, coincides with that other modern fashion of depreciating its utility, and both are phases of that ever-encroaching sacerdotalism of our time which is hostile to free inquiry into Church history or to a free use of the human reason in matters of doctrine. But a Protestant Christian who holds aloof from that vortex, and looks, with the complacency of a landsman on the toilers of the sea, upon the frivolities of theological controversy and upon the anathemas of the sects, may still assert the same freedom to form his opinion about the Fathers as about the Popes, and to scrutinise the primitive as closely as the mediæval Church. And from that standpoint it is necessary to refer briefly to the general history of the Catholic Church, in order to justify the conclusions suggested by the subsequent comparison between her teaching and the teaching of Philosophy.

It has long been a matter of general admission that, from the very infancy of the Church, questions of dogma and discipline came to be of paramount importance, whilst purity of life and action fell into a secondary position. A man's Christianity was measured less by his works than by his faith; and to think wrongly about the Trinity was soon esteemed more unchristian than to deal wrongly with a neighbour. Consequently the history of the Church became and remained the history of its extreme and more illiterate section; and, though in its turgid stream there always flowed a thin streak of the truer

Christianity, and of the spirit of its Founder, the gentler and more rational votaries of the new religion were too few or too weak to affect either its colour or its character; they either kept in the background or became outcasts and heretics. The fanatics carried all before them, and Christianity came to be represented in history, not by the more tolerant and liberal spirit of Origen, Hosius of Cordova, Synesius, Paul of Samosata, Vigilantius, or Pelagius, men who in becoming Christians still continued to recognise and retain the virtues of Paganism, but by the narrow, intolerant spirit which has made the names of Tertullian, Athanasius, Augustine, Jerome, Dominic, or Torquemada a disgrace, no less to human nature itself, than to the religion they so shamefully misconstrued and perverted. Whether the world would have fared any better had men of this latter type never been produced, no one of course can say with certitude; but I need not suppress my humble but strong conviction in favour of the opinion that it would.

The progress of the Church, till at least quite recent times, has ever been one uninterrupted triumph over the Broad Church or Rational school. Since the days when the bones of Origen were exhumed for imputed heresy—one of the most hateful incidents in the annals of orthodoxy—the more liberal school of theology has been in a constant minority. The purer ideas of the Divine attributes held by Marcion gave way before the bad reasoning of Tertullian. The protests of Jovinian and Vigilantius against the abuses of monasticism and relic-worship were drowned in the torrent of Jerome's vituperation. The more rational conclusions of Pelagius succumbed to the narrow notions of Augustine; whilst Cyril of Alexandria achieved an easy victory over his intellectual superior, Nestorius. Of course had it been otherwise, had the broader spirit prevailed, the history of Catholicism might have been, and no doubt would have been, a less appalling narrative than it is; but for purposes of comparison we must take facts as they are, nor seek to blink their significance by arbitrarily representing what is bad therein as only illustrative of the abuses, and not of the essence, of Catholicism as a factor in history.

Looking, however, in this way at the history of the Catholic Church as a whole, and perceiving therein between the spirit of Christ and the spirit of historical Christianity a difference amounting to absolute antithesis, I am free to doubt the extent of the benefit claimed for the world as a consequence of the triumph of the Church under Constantine and Theodosius, and to dispute the moral revolution said to have been effected by the final overthrow of Philosophy under Justinian. The problem is one chiefly of historical speculation, the interest of which is at least equalled by its complexity, and on which one cannot look for any unanimity of conclusion. I merely indicate the impression enforced by some study of the subject upon my own mind. But a similar impression must have been made upon Dean Milman, when he wrote that "in a great degree, while the Roman world became Christian in outward worship and in faith, it remained heathen, or even at some periods worse than heathen in its better times, as to beneficence, gentleness, purity, social virtue, humanity, and peace." Which I may translate into the plain statement, that Christianity in the form it came to assume did not improve in any essential respects the general state of the world.

Turning next to the contrast between the literature of Paganism and that of the Church, no one can read the works of the Fathers without perceiving at once that he has passed, not merely from an altogether different, but to an altogether lower, intellectual atmosphere. Painful to the last degree is the change from Cicero or Seneca to Tertullian or Augustine. It is like the change from Italian sunlight to an English fog. The calm, sober argument, the clear thought, the graceful expression, where are they? Gone, gone for ages from the enjoyment of men; and their place taken by tedious prolixity, uncouth language, and by a logic that would be contemptible in a child. By reason of that mental servility—in itself the strongest proof of mental inferiority—which led most of them to accept without criticism the letter of any Scripture, provided it were from Palestine, all the more important arguments of the Fathers simply begged the question in dispute, all their interpretations of prophecy revolved in a vicious circle. Such and such an event was foretold by such and such a prophecy, because such and such a prophecy foretold, or might be twisted into foretelling, such and such an event! Never did their arguments on prophecy rise above this level; but of the sheer irrationality to which they often descended let a single illustration from Tertullian suffice. He is seeking to explain to the Jews the meaning of the passage: "His glory is of a bull, his horns the horn of a unicorn: with them shall he push the nations together into the very extremity of the earth" (Deut. xxxiii. 17). A man of common sense would reject the passage at once as utterly unintelligible, or as applicable to any great conqueror who had troubled the nations; but with Tertullian the bull must needs mean Christ, and the horns of the bull the extremities of that Cross wherewith he then was tossing all nations through faith, wafting them from earth to heaven, as he would in future toss them through judgment, casting them down from heaven to earth! Nothing could surely be sillier than this, though, if not surpassed, it is at least matched in the thirty-second chapter of the eighteenth book of the *City of God*, by Augustine, sometimes called, and quite possibly with truth, the *most* philosophical of the Fathers.

Refraining, however, from further illustrations of the mental calibre of the Fathers, who from their fear of thinking freely lapsed into thinking badly, I must also express the opinion that between them and the Philosophers there is a moral no less than an intellectual abyss; that is to say, that a man may derive more mental and spiritual profit, higher aspirations for virtue, toleration, and humanity, from Seneca or Marcus Aurelius than from writers like Augustine and Tertullian. The moral teaching of the Pagans is on a purer and higher level than that of the Fathers, just as the lives of the Pagans, Praetextatus, Themistius, or Libanius, rise far above those of their leading Christian contemporaries.

In short, the conviction under which the following pages were written, and which they are meant to enforce, is, that the triumph over Paganism of that type of Christianity which issued from the cauldron of theological strife as the only really orthodox form; which became stereotyped in Roman Catholicism; which produced the Crusades, the religious orders, and the Inquisition; and which is now striving to assert its blighting supremacy over Protestant Christianity, has been, not a gain, but a misfortune, to the world, and has retarded rather than promoted civilisation.

CONTENTS

CHAPTER I

PAGAN MONOTHEISM

Monotheism not confined to Judaea—Antiquity of theism in Greece—Polytheism overthrown by Philosophy—Theistic phrases in common use among the Pagans—High attributes of the Deity in Pagan theology—The doctrine of plurality in unity—Admission by Arnobius of extra-Christian monotheism—Hymn of Aristides to Jupiter—Origen's failure to answer Celsus—His appeal to magic on behalf of the Christians—His belief in the animate life of the sun, moon, and stars—Theism as taught by Seneca and Cicero—Pagan arguments for theism from design in nature—Contrast between Hellenic and Hebraic theology—High theological ideas of Celsus—Deductions from the monotheism of the early Christians—The worship of angels and martyrs—The Pagan theory of demons—Angels, demons, and gods used as convertible terms—Polytheistic language of St. Clement and St. Augustine—Polytheistic belief of the early Christians—Polytheism of the Jews—The Christian polemic against the Pagan mythology inferior to that of the Philosophers 1

CHAPTER II

PAGAN THEOLOGY

International character of ancient religion—Universal belief in Providence—Seneca's treatise on Providence—Epictetus on the same—Providential government through angels or demons—The Pagan theory of the guardian angel—Maximus of Tyre on the problem of evil—Maximus of Tyre on prayer—Pagan prayer for spiritual as well as temporal blessings—Seneca and Cicero on the highest mode of worship—The place of prayer in Pagan life—Marcus Aurelius on the due length of prayer—The prayer of Simplicius, the last philosopher 29

CHAPTER III

PAGAN RELIGION

Belief in the goodness of God the first principle in the religion of Philosophy—Man's duty towards God as taught by Epictetus—Resignation to the Divine Will: taught alike by Pagans and Christians—Religious sentiments of Epictetus and Marcus Aurelius—Seneca and Porphyry on the imitation of God—High Pagan ideas of attainable moral perfection contrasted with Christian in their effects on conduct—Seneca on the equality between a good man and Jupiter—The Stoic theory of close relationship between God and man—The universal presence of God—The conscience as the vicegerent of God—Language of the Fathers on human equality with God—Porphyry's letter to Marcella—General religious sentiment of Paganism—Fragmentary nature of Pagan literature—Eclectic philosophy—Justice done by Zwingli to ancient religion and philosophy 45

CHAPTER IV

PAGAN SUPERSTITION

The forces of scepticism and superstition in antiquity—Plutarch on superstition and atheism—Rapid propagation of Oriental religions in Rome—Character of the mysteries of Isis and Osiris—Persecution futile against foreign religions

—Spread of Jewish superstitions in Rome—Pagan ascetic rites condemned by Seneca—A good as well as a bad side to the mysteries—Baptism and purificatory rites in the mysteries—The mysteries as teaching a future life—Allegorical meaning of absurd customs in the mysteries—Allegorical interpretation of Greek mythology—Allegorical interpretation of the books of Moses by later Jews, and by the Christian school at Alexandria—Illustrations of explanations of Jewish prophecies—Pagan prototypes of the Hermits and Flagellants—The higher Pagan feeling concerning temples and sacrifices—The Pagan defence of idolatry—Maximus of Tyre on the true meaning of idolatry—Seneca's ideas about sacrifices—Apollonius of Tyana on the same—Sacrifice in Catholic theory and practice—Comparison between Catholic and Pagan superstition . . 71

CHAPTER V

THE PAGAN BELIEF IN HEAVEN

Pagan theory of the soul—Its Divine origin and destiny—The Stoic doctrine of the brotherhood of all men—Origen's testimony to the good influence of Philosophy—The body as the prison of the soul—The soul destined to return to God and heaven—Antiquity of the belief in the soul's immortality—Cicero's faith in a future life—Seneca and Plutarch on the same—Seneca's consolation to Marcia—Apotheosis and canonisation—Vividness of Pagan belief in a second life—Christian opposition to Pagan belief in immortality—Future life as a reward for virtue—General Pagan disbelief in a corporeal resurrection—Christian allegorical acceptance of resurrection—Catholic dogma of the damnation of unbaptized infants—No similar superstition in Paganism 91

CHAPTER VI

THE PAGAN BELIEF IN HELL

Pre-Christian belief in Hell universal—Pagan belief in everlasting future punishments: proved by words of Celsus and

Plutarch—The idea popularised by art and by the stage—
Plutarch's dream of Thespesius—Plato, Zeno, and Lucian
on future punishment—Christian admission of identity of
Pagan belief with their own—The belief intensified by
Catholicism, which counteracted the efforts of Philosophy
against it—Philosophical denial or figurative explanation
of Hell—Pagan conceptions of death: illustrated from
Cicero, Epictetus, and Marcus Aurelius—St. Augustine on
the nature of Hell-fire—Also Lactantius, Minucius Felix,
and Cyprian—Heretical views of Origen and John Erigena
—Fierce intolerance of Tertullian—Christianity degraded
by the Church Fathers—The real origin of the idea of Hell
as shown by comparative mythology and folk-lore . . 108

CHAPTER VII

THE END OF THE WORLD

Stoic belief in the final conflagration of the world—Seneca's
firm expectation of an end to the world—Similarity between Pagan, Jewish, and Persian ideas—The idea due to
imperfect state of physical science—Oriental expectation
of a great liberator: and of a mighty Oriental empire—
Josephus on the expectations of the Jews—Jewish hope of
overthrowing the Roman Empire: inherited by the
Christians—The millennium a principal belief of the
early Church—No real difference between early Christian
and Jewish expectations—Sensual ideas of millennium in
Irenaeus—Vision of the New Jerusalem—Political aspect
of the millennium—End of the Roman Empire looked for
by the Christians: and threatened in literature of forged
prophecies—Insulting language applied to Rome—Catholicism acceptable for its hatred of Rome—Coincidence of
the virtual downfall of Rome with the date predicted
by the Church—Persecution of the Catholics mainly political—Simplicity of the test of loyalty to the empire—
Value of Christian apologies against disaffection—Christianity regarded as a treasonable conspiracy—Roman intolerance otherwise unaccountable 129

CONTENTS xvii

CHAPTER VIII

PAGAN PHILOSOPHY

PAGE

Did Catholicism inaugurate a moral revolution ?—Two sides to early Christian character—Influence of Antinomianism in the early Church—Tertullian's evidence of the bad state of the Church : confirmed by Cyprian, Salvian, and Aristides—The wide and good influence of Philosophy—Philosophy as the culture of the soul—The province of Philosophy : co-extensive with religion and morality—Philosophical lectures and missions—The duty of self-improvement—The duty of self-examination—The duty to conscience—The real punishment of sin—Virtue as its own reward—Contrast with Christian ideas—Seneca's ideal Stoic—Justinian's closing of schools of Philosophy at Athens—The glacial period of human intelligence . . 151

CHAPTER IX

PAGAN MORALITY

Influence of self-sacrifice in antiquity—Seneca on living for others—Philosophy more cosmopolitan than Catholicism—The fraternity of mankind a Stoic idea—Teaching of Zeno and Epictetus—The Pagan duty of charity—Seneca on unselfish beneficence—Seneca on the etiquette of charity—Care of the poor in Pagan societies—State charity in Athens and Rome—The Pagan duty of forgiveness—The Pagan duty of toleration—Extracts from Seneca's treatise *On Anger*—Real spirit of Stoicism—The Philosophers more Christian than the Fathers 172

CHAPTER X

CHRISTIANITY AND CIVILISATION

(1) Improvement in domestic life—Catholic disregard for family ties—(2) Christianity in relation to slavery—Move-

ment against it of Pagan origin—Stories of the slave system—Seneca on duty to slaves—(3) Christianity and the gladiatorial games—Salvian's explanation of their cessation—Pagan opposition to them—(4) Abolition of human sacrifices—The chief triumph of Roman civilisation —(5) Christianity and cruelty to animals—(6) Christianity and cruelty of punishments and torture—(7) Christianity in regard to war—Modern progress a return to principles of Philosophy 193

CONCLUSION 221

APPENDIX 231

CHAPTER I

PAGAN MONOTHEISM

THE basis of theological belief affords an interesting starting-point for comparison between Christianity and Paganism. For the burden of the writings of all the early Christian Fathers who defended their faith against the Pagan theology was that, whereas they only worshipped one God, their opponents worshipped many. Sometimes, indeed, as in the case of Justin Martyr, Lactantius, or Clemens of Alexandria, they would appeal in their arguments or apologies to classical literature itself in favour of monotheism; but they upheld monotheism nevertheless as the leading point of difference between the Christian and Pagan schools of thought, and the doctrine of the divinity of Christ, if traceable at all, was regarded by them as a matter of quite secondary importance compared with the remonstrance they saw fit to make with the absurdities of polytheism and the worship of idols.

And from that time to this it has always been asserted or implied that at the birth of Christianity there was, outside the Jewish race, either no belief in nor knowledge of God at all, or no idea of His real attributes.

But nothing could be farther from the truth. The Pagan world was by no means in that state of theological darkness which the early Christian missionaries, ignorant for the most part of Greek or Roman literature and philosophy, imagined or believed. The theological difference between the new faith and the old touched rather the surface than the substance of thought; nor is there a single attribute now ascribed to the Deity that the tomb-inscriptions of Egypt do not prove to have been ascribed to Him fully 6000 years ago.

To the conception of the unity of God nothing was added by Christianity that had not for centuries before been familiar to the educated classes of the world. The Fathers themselves sometimes admitted this, as when Tertullian says that the greater part of the human race, though they knew not even the name of Moses, yet knew the God of Moses.[1]

But the admission requires some supplementary proof from a glance at the vast mass of evidence contained in classical literature.

The conception of God as the formative or crea-

[1] *Against Marcion*, i. 10.

tive power of the universe was present in the very infancy of Greek thought; for though Thales, the earliest Greek philosopher, and famous for his conjecture that water was the beginning of all things, is declared by St. Augustine to have had no idea of a divine mind ruling the world, and is classed by Clement among the atheists, we have the prior and better evidence of both Cicero and Plutarch that he also postulated the existence of God, who formed all things out of water.[1] But probably he only availed himself of an idea that was already current in his time; his speculation about water as the origin of things, like those of others about air or fire, referring rather to the mode of the formation of nature than to its creation, and no more excluding the idea of God than did the physical speculations of Descartes or Laplace. If Anaxagoras were really the originator of the idea in Greek philosophy, how was it that such a saying was attributed to Thales as that God was the most ancient of all things, inasmuch as He had no birth, and that the world was the most beautiful of all things because it was the work of God?[2]

The idea was never afterwards absent from Greek philosophy, and the fundamental unity of the Deity

[1] Compare the *City of God*, viii. 3, and Clement's *Exhortation to the Heathen*, v., with Cicero's *De Natura Deorum*, i. 10, and Plutarch's *Opinions of Philosophers*, 7. Athenagoras, *Apol.* 23, admits the recognition by Thales of God as the intelligence of the world.

[2] Diogenes Laertius, *Lives of the Philosophers*, i. 9.

was affirmed as clearly by Xenophanes, Parmenides, Plato, Sophocles, and others, as by any writer of the Hebrew race. " God is one," taught the Pythagoreans, " the giver of light in heaven, and the Father of all, the mind and vital power of the world, the mover of all things."

The same teaching ruled not merely in the schools of philosophy, but in poetry and on the stage. " One is God, one," wrote Sophocles, " who made both the heaven and the far-stretching earth and the ocean's blue wave and the mighty winds";[1] and even Diphilus, the comic poet, had for a line—

<blockquote>Father of all, to Him alone incessant reverence pay.</blockquote>

To reproduce all the evidence of this sort would be an endless task, and the frequent confirmation of it in the sequel renders it unnecessary; suffice it to say, that it amply confirms the admission of an early Christian apocryphal work, attributed by Clement of Alexandria to St. Peter, to the effect that the Greeks worshipped the same God as the Christians, and that the only difference between them lay in the manner, not in the object, of their worship.[2] The notion favoured by the early Fathers—Origen, Clement, Justin Martyr, and Ambrose—that there existed a Greek translation of the Pentateuch prior

---

[1] Clemens, *Stromata*, v. 14; Athenagoras and Justin Martyr also quote the passage, and the doubts thrown on its authenticity seem uncalled for. [2] *Ib.* vi. 5.

to the Septuagint version, and that thence Plato and other Greek thinkers became familiar with the theology of the Hebrews, need only be mentioned to be rejected as entirely destitute of evidence.

Philosophy, in fact, achieved its aim. It purified Zeus or Jupiter from all the gross stories of the popular mythology or folk-lore; it propagated the conception of one Supreme Beneficent Deity; and it reduced the multitude of other gods either into so many phases or attributes of the Deity or into allegorical interpretations of Nature. It established, in short, a rational theology out of the crudest possible materials.

Hence it came to pass that from an early time the terms Zeus, Jupiter, and God became convertible, connoting the same ideas. "The knowledge of one God is possessed by all," Tertullian admits; and he quotes such phrases in common use among the Pagans as " God sees," " God knows," " Good God," " I commend you to God," " God is good," " As God will," to show their essential belief in one sole Deity, above and beyond all other gods.[1]

Cyprian and Minucius Felix also allude to the frequent employment of the same name by the common people in similar phrases;[2] and Lactantius calls

---

[1] *De Testimonio Animae*, 2; *Apologeticus*, 17; *Resurrectio Carnis*, 3; *De Anima*, 42.
[2] Cyprian, *Vanity of Idols*, 9; Felix, *Octavius*, 18.

special attention to the fact that on occasions of thanksgiving or of distress, as in time of war, pestilence, drought, or poverty, the language of praise or prayer was raised directly to God, by name, and not to Jupiter.[1] Hence it is idle to talk of Theism as confined in pre-Christian times to the philosophical few; language proves it to have been universal.

This evidence of early Christian writers bears witness to the fundamental agreement between Christian and pre-Christian thought on the first article of theology. But the agreement applied not only to the name, but to the very attributes of Divinity. This is proved by such common expressions as "God is good," "God is great," or "God is true." Cornutus the Stoic derived Zeus, the world-ruling soul, either from σώζειν, "to Save," or from ζῆν, "to Live," according as God might be thought of as the Saviour of men or as the First Cause of Life.[2] It was as the cause of the generation or preservation of all things that He was called the common Father of men and gods, and Dion Chrysostom named Him the great King of kings, as Seneca named Him the God of gods. Plutarch and Pindar, no less than Isaiah (xlv. 21) applied to Him the term *Saviour*, and by this title it was common to address Him in prayer, as we

---

[1] *Divine Institutes*, ii. 1. Compare the *Clementine Recognitions*, v. 30, where St. Peter alludes to the Pagan custom of praying for rain to Almighty God, and not to images, in time of drought.

[2] *De Natura Deorum*, 11.

know from the prayer of Simplicius, the last of the philosophers, at the end of his commentary on the *Manual* of Epictetus. He was also the Father of Justice, Equity, and Peace;[1] and among his many epithets was that of Gracious or Merciful (μείλιχος), from His readiness to become reconciled to men as soon as they turned them from the ways of injustice.[2]

One cannot protest too often against the supposition that these ideas were confined to the few, and that Pagan society generally was not impregnated with them. The language of the stage and of common life is conclusive to the contrary. It proves too much to say that a plurality of gods continued to be recognised in a thousand ways, for even the higher writers, like Plutarch or Seneca or Plato, whose monotheistic belief was often expressed without doubt, continued to speak of the "gods," or, even if they used the singular number, often used it generically, as we use the word man as a synonym for all men. This they did partly from force of habit, and partly from their wish to purify the popular theology without openly assailing or offending it; and puzzling as it may often be to us to meet in the same paragraph or even in the same sentence with the words God or Gods used as con-

---

[1] Plutarch, *Contradictions of Stoics*, 32.
[2] Cornutus, *De Natura Deorum*, 11.

vertible terms, the polytheism of the language of the writers need not conceal from us the real monotheism of their meaning.

Thus in the time of Sylla, the Latin poet Valerius Soranus wrote of Jupiter the following lines :—

> Jupiter omnipotens, rerum rex, ipse Deusque,
> Progenitor genetrixque, Deûm Deus, *unus et omnes.*

And long before his time, Janus, who then occupied the place in Roman theology afterwards accorded to Jupiter, was addressed in the hymns of the Salii as Deorum Deus;[1] so that the expression God of gods was a Pagan before it became a Christian one, and Jew, Christian, and Pagan meant the same thing when they spoke of the Deity as *Supreme.* The conception of plurality in unity practically identified monotheism and polytheism. The Christian doctrine of trinity in unity renders the earlier conception intelligible.

And how easy it was for educated men to reconcile their belief in one God with time-honoured traditions by explaining the several gods as the different manifestations of the First Cause and Creator of all things! Bacchus, Hercules, or Mercury were so many synonyms for God, according to Seneca; the name Bacchus referring to Him as the parent of all things, the name Hercules referring to

[1] Macrobius, *Saturnalia,* i. 9.

His insuperable power, and the name Mercury referring to Him as the source of reason, numbers, order, and knowledge.[1] Or what can be clearer than Maximus of Tyre, when he says of the gods that though their names are many, their nature is one, and that we only from our ignorance call them by different names, just as, though there is really only one sea, we speak of the Aegean, Ionian, or Cretan seas?[2]

These ideas were common property in the days when philosophy permeated every class of society, down even to the very slaves, as we know from the cases of Epictetus and Phaedo. The words of the grammarian, Maximus of Madaura, in his letter to St. Augustine, may be taken to express the almost universal attitude of Pagan thought: "That there is one Supreme God, without beginning or posterity, that there is a great and glorious Father, who is so mad or so prejudiced as to deny as a most certain truth? His virtues, scattered through the work of creation, we invoke under many names, because we are all of us ignorant of His real name. For God is a name common to all religions . . . Who is that God of yours, of whom you Christians claim, as it

---

[1] *De Beneficiis*, iv. 8. Compare Diogenes Laertius, vii. 62, where Minerva, Juno, Vulcan, Neptune, and Ceres are all mentioned as synonyms of God, according to different attributes of His nature, in the philosophy of the Stoics.

[2] *Dissertation* xxxix. 5.

were, the exclusive possession and first discovery?"[1]

St. Augustine, in his ill-tempered reply, forgot or was unable to answer the main question of his correspondent.

But there exists no stronger admission of the widely-spread monotheistic thought of Paganism than is afforded by one of the ablest of the Christian apologists in the midst of a polemic against the old mythology, in which he, like others of his school, was simply slaying what had been twice or thrice slain by philosophy. "Who," asks Arnobius, "is that one God? Perhaps we, instructed by true authority, might say; but lest you should not be willing to believe us, let my opponent ask the Egyptians, Persians, Indians, Chaldeans, Armenians . . . then you will learn who is that one God, and who the very many under Him are who pretend to be gods and make sport of man's ignorance."[2]

When therefore the Pagans, in answer to the charges of the Christians, declared that in their use of the term Jupiter they were really at one with the Christians and meant the same thing, the latter had no effective reply. To object to the identification, as Arnobius did, on the ground that Jupiter had

---

[1] "Quis sit iste Deus, quem vobis Christiani quasi primum vindicatis?" etc.   [2] *Adversus Gentes*, iv. 13.

parents, grandparents, and other relations, and that therefore he could not be called everlasting,[1] was altogether disingenuous, for he must have known that the Jupiter of the later Roman religion had long ceased to have anything in common but the name with the Jupiter or Zeus of the primitive mythology. The hymn to Jupiter by Aristides the Sophist (176 A.D.) may be quoted in proof: "Jupiter made all things; all things whatever are the works of Jupiter,—rivers, and the earth, and the sea, and the heaven, and whatever is between or above, or beneath them; and gods, and men, and all living things, and all things visible or intelligible. First of all He made Himself; nor was He ever brought up in the caverns of Crete; nor did Saturn ever intend to devour Him; nor did He swallow a stone in His stead; nor was Jupiter ever in any danger, nor will He ever be. . . . But He is the First, and the most ancient, and the Prince of all things, and Himself from Himself." This single quotation is an answer to half the criticisms of the Fathers against the Pagan theology.

But less satisfactory even than such criticism as that indulged in by Arnobius was the answer of Origen to Celsus. The latter urged that it made no difference whether the Supreme Being (ὁ ὕψιστος) were called Zeus, or Zen, or Adonai, or Sabaoth, or

[1] *Adversus Gentes*, i. 34.

Ammoun, or Pappaeus, if all the people who used these names meant identically the same thing. But Origen insisted that the Christians were right in struggling even to death to avoid calling God Zeus, although he could adduce no better reason than a gross superstition from the philosophy of magic! The names of one language, he contended, had no longer the same power when translated into another; so that, for instance, an incantation that might be performed on a Roman name could not be performed on the same name in Greek, and conversely! If, then, that was the case even with the names of men, what must it not be with those of the Deity? An invocation or oath, therefore, by the God of Abraham, or of Isaac, or of Jacob, would produce a result that would fail with other names; and the word Sabaoth, so potent in incantations, would accomplish nothing when translated into Lord of Hosts or Almighty. It was for reasons such as these that Christians were and should be ready to suffer anything rather than admit an identity between Jupiter and God![1]

Nothing surely could be weaker than this; or again, than Origen's answer to Celsus, on the ground of the irreverence shown by the Christians to the heavenly luminaries, which so many of the ancients regarded or worshipped as actual gods. "Being per-

---

[1] *Against Celsus*, i. 25 and v. 41.

suaded," he says, "that the sun himself, and the moon, and stars pray to the Supreme God through His only-begotten Son, we think it improper to pray to these beings who themselves offer prayers to God, seeing even they themselves would prefer we should send up prayers to the God to whom they pray, rather than send them down to themselves or distribute our power of prayer between God and themselves."[1] Evidently therefore Christians on the intellectual level of Origen regarded the luminaries, if not as gods, yet as animated beings; so that on this point there was no fundamental divergence between themselves and their opponents.

In those days, just as in our own, the world was divided between theistic, atheistic, and agnostic schools of thought; nor has Christianity added anything to the following argument of Seneca against the Epicurean theory of the indifference of God to the welfare of mankind: "God confers no benefits!" he exclaims. "Whence, then, all the things that you possess? ... Whence all those countless objects that delight your eyes, your ears, your mind? Whence all that bounty that furnishes you with luxury, seeing that it is not only our necessities that have been provided for, but that love is shown to us, even to our

---

[1] *Against Celsus*, v. 11. Compare viii. 67 : ὑμνουμέν γε θεὸν καὶ τὸν Μονογενῆ αὐτοῦ, ὡς καὶ ἥλιος καὶ σελήνη καὶ ἄστρα καὶ πᾶσα ἡ οὐρανία στρατιά, etc.

most fanciful wants?... And when what you have you highly prize, you are so ungrateful as to say you owe it to no one! Whence have you that breath you breathe, or that light by which you dispose and order the actions of your life, or the coursing blood that sustains your vital heat?... It is Nature, you say, which bestows these things upon man. But do you not perceive that in saying Nature you but give another name to God, for what else is Nature than God and the divine reason that pervades the world in whole and part? You may at your pleasure call by any other appellation the Author of the things we see, and may rightly address Him as Jupiter the Best and Greatest, or Jupiter the Thunderer, or Jupiter the Stator, and Stabilitor, so called, not, as historians have handed it down, because in accordance with prayer He caused the Roman army to stay its flight, but because through His goodness all things stay firm and stand. Nor if you also call Him Fate will you speak amiss; for since Fate is nothing else than a complicated series of causes, He is the First Cause of all, on which all other causes depend. Whatever names you please will be fitting, provided they connote some of the force and influence of heavenly things: His names may be as numerous as his attributes... To no purpose, then, most ungrateful of mortals, do you deny your debt to God but admit your debt to Nature, for neither is

Nature without God, nor God without Nature, for they are identical and have the same functions.... Call Him Nature, Fate, Chance—all are names for the same God in the various manifestations of His power."[1]

There is not the smallest proof that Seneca was a Christian, nor that he ever saw St. Paul at Rome. The Christian who forged a correspondence between him and the Apostle forged it in vain. Seneca simply expressed the common opinions of his day, with which the Stoics more especially had made the world familiar, in a literature of which unfortunately little more than fragments remain. And at all events no suspicion of Christian influence can rest upon Cicero, who in sentiment is as much a Christian as Seneca. "What so plain and evident," he makes a Stoic say, "when we look up at the sky and contemplate the heavens, as that there is a Divinity of surpassing intelligence who governs them?"[2]

And as the argument from Nature was as complete in the hands of the Pagan philosophers as it has ever been since, so was the argument from Design or the argument from the Universal Belief of mankind. "Who, then, is it," asks Epictetus, "that has fitted this to that and that to this; that has fitted the sheath to the sword and the sword to the sheath? Is it no one? From the very construction of per-

[1] *De Beneficiis*, iv. 5. [2] *De Natura Deorum*, ii. 2.

fected things we are wont to show that the work is of some workman and not constructed to no purpose, and does each of these things demonstrate the workman, but visible things and sight and light not demonstrate that other?" And for the other argument: "The strongest reason to be adduced," says Cicero, "for our belief in the gods seems to be that no people is so savage, no single man so monstrous, as not to have their or his mind embued with a notion of the gods."[1] Or Seneca : " We deduce the existence of the gods from this among other reasons, that all men have an innate conception of them, and that no race of men has ever been so far removed from all legal and moral restraint as not to believe in the gods."[2]

The supreme merit of Pagan philosophy lies in the transition it effected from the more primitive notion of the stupendous might of God to that of His superhuman goodness and beneficence. This change or advance of thought the world owes far more to the Greeks than to the Hebrews ; a fact, in the history of theology, which has only failed to be recognised by reason of the long persistence of the idea that the Jews, a small branch of the whole human family, were in a more special sense than other members of that family the objects of the divine love and solicitude. Now that we recognise the moral and intel-

[1] *Tusc. Quaest.* i. 13.   [2] *Epist.* 117.

lectual necessity of regarding Jews, Greeks, Romans, and others as all equal in the eyes of Him, whom all alike addressed as their Father, we are able to see that, in regard to the attributes of Divinity, the Greeks and Romans were at least on a level with, and on many points in advance of, the Jews; and the debt of the Hellenising Jews to the Greeks is beyond all comparison in excess of any we know of as due from the Greek race to the Hebrew.

Marcion, the Christian, from his inability to reconcile the Jehovah of the Old Testament with his idea of perfect goodness, postulated the existence of another and greater God, to whom Jehovah occupied a subordinate position; and many other of the early heretics did the same. Plutarch actually refers to the Jews and Syrians as forming exceptions to the general belief of mankind in the goodness of the gods and their kindness to men.[1] One of the most famous passages in Plato is where he argues that God, as being good, can only be the Cause of good, not of bad; and Maximus of Tyre, in discussing the origin of evil, protests vehemently against connecting it with God: "Not from Heaven, by Zeus, not from Heaven!"[2] Seneca well expressed the conclusion of Roman theology when he wrote: "No man in his senses fears the gods, for it were madness to fear what is good for us, nor does any one fear whom he

[1] *Contradictions of Stoics*, 38.   [2] *Dissertation* xli. 2.

loves"; or again: "By the aid of Philosophy we shall neither fear death nor the gods; we shall know that neither is death an evil, nor the gods bad"; or lastly: "What cause constrains the gods to confer blessings on us? Their nature. It is a mistake to think they have not the will to do injury—they have not the power; they can neither feel injury nor inflict it."[1]

Clearly we are here in as different an atmosphere as possible from that of the older Pagan or Hebrew theology. Any one, indeed, can see that there is more difference between the earlier and later Paganism than between the latter and Christianity. The following extracts may fitly conclude this part of the subject:—

"God is the God of all, good, and in need of nothing, and without jealousy."

"We must in no wise ever lose our hold of God, neither by day nor night, neither in public nor in private, neither in word nor deed; but whatever we do, let the soul always be directed to God."

"Should any worshipper of God be commanded to do anything impious, or say anything base, such command should in no wise ever be obeyed, but we must rather bear any kind of torture or submit to any kind of death before we not merely say but even think anything unholy about God."

These extracts are from no Christian Father, nor

---

[1] *De Beneficiis*, iv. 19; *Epist.*, 75, 95.

from any Christian at all, but from Celsus, the anti-Christian philosopher, who wrote a book against the new religion, to which Origen replied, with arguments less remarkable, it must be admitted, for their relevancy than for their length. And the same high conception of the Supreme Deity was upheld by other Pagan writers, who, like Hierocles or Longinian, either took an active part in opposition to Christianity or declined to recognise any fundamental novelty in its theology. In the face of persistent misrepresentation of the past, it is only fair to restate these facts, which of course have no bearing whatever on the more rational Christianity of our own day, but which have a good deal on the Christianity of the early Catholic Church, as established and interpreted by the Fathers.

The question may next be hazarded whether the difference between the Christians and the Pagans was so very great with regard to the actual worship of a plurality of gods; whether, in fact, the monotheism of the early Christians has not been as much overstated as the polytheism of the Pagans. Certain it is that St. Ambrose advocated the direct invocation of angels and martyrs as intermediaries between God and man;[1] and the prohibition of angelolatry by the Synod of Laodicea in the fourth century indicates at

---

[1] *De Viduis*, ix. 55 : Obsecrandi sunt angeli qui nobis ad praesidium dati sunt : martyres obsecrandi, etc.

all events the common practice and belief of the many. The adoption of Christianity did not necessarily involve even the forsaking of actual idols, for Salvian speaks of an idol in Africa which not only the Pagans but the Christians worshipped in the fourth century, when all persecution of Christianity was over.[1] But, idolatry apart, it is clear that the martyrs and angels simply took the place of the old gods and heroes, not merely in the position they were supposed to occupy towards mankind, but in every detail of the service and reverence that mankind was expected to pay to them. St. Augustine's answer to this charge made by Faustus, the Manichaean, is not borne out by an inquiry into the Christian customs of his time. But polytheism for polytheism, that of the Church lacked the poetical charm of the earlier form ; whilst mythology for mythology, the legends of the saints were at best an indifferent substitute for the legends of the gods and heroes.

Then again we have to remember that there is nothing intrinsically irrational in the polytheistic theory itself, and that it matters less, the Pagans would have argued, in how many gods people believe

[1] viii. Quis enim non eorum qui Christiani appellantur coelestem illum, aut post Christum adoravit aut, quod est pejus, multo ante quam Christum ? Compare Theodoret, *ad Col.* ii. 18, iii. 17. Theodoret mentions Phrygia and Pisidia as the headquarters of angelolatry. Their view coincided exactly with the Platonic one, that it was only through angels that there could be any mediation or intercourse between God and man.

than in what kind of moral attributes they attach to Divinity. Plato and his followers therefore are blameless if, conceiving that the purely spiritual and emotionless nature of God precluded Him from direct action upon this world of matter, they imagined a hierarchy of beneficent beings, called demons, partaking of the divine nature by reason of their immortality, and of the human nature by reason of their subjection to emotions, and fitted therefore to act as intermediaries between earth and heaven, between God and man.[1] Maximus of Tyre describes them as a link between human weakness and divine beauty, as bridging over the gulf between mortal and immortal, and as acting between gods and men as interpreters acted between Greeks and barbarians. He calls them secondary gods ($\theta\epsilon o\grave{\iota}$ $\delta\epsilon\acute{u}\tau\epsilon\rho o\iota$), and speaks of them as the departed souls of virtuous men ("the spirits of just men made perfect," the Christian would have said), appointed by God to overrule every part of human life, by helping the good, avenging the injured, and punishing the unjust. Among other characteristics, he speaks of them as messengers of unseen things ($\mathring{a}\gamma\gamma\epsilon\lambda o\iota$ $\tau\hat{\omega}\nu$ $\mathring{a}\phi a\nu\hat{\omega}\nu$);[2] and Plutarch too calls them messengers or *angels* between gods and men, and describes them as the spies of the former, wandering at their commands, punishing wrong-doers and guarding the course of

[1] Apuleius, *De Deo Socratis*, 674.   [2] *Diss.* 14, 15.

the virtuous.¹ So that angels and demons were convertible terms among the Pagans; and their polytheism was nothing more than angelolatry.

It was these demons, according to Apuleius, who as gods (*divorum numero*) were in Egypt pleased with lamentations, or in Greece with dances, and to whom all religious rites were paid.² In short, it was into demons, for the most part beneficent, that the gods were resolved, and the words gods, demons, or angels, with Christian no less than Pagan writers, came to be used as synonymous terms. Origen identifies gods, angels of God, good demons, and heroes, and refers to passages in the Psalms to show that angels were sometimes spoken of as gods.³ Arnobius speaks of "gods, angels, demons, or whatever else their name."⁴ Augustine refers to those called gods by the philosophers as identical with beings whom the Christians called angels.⁵ And Lactantius, in reference to Seneca's account of ministers set by God over the world, only contends for the word messengers or angels as a preferable term, while protesting against their being called or worshipped as gods; and he quotes an oracle of Apollo, in which the gods were called the messengers or angels of God.⁶

---

¹ *Cessation of Oracles*, 13, and *Face in Orb of the Moon*, 30.
² *De Deo Socratis*, 684.   ³ *Against Celsus*, ii. 37, and v. 4.
⁴ ii. 35.   ⁵ *City of God*, xix. 3.   ⁶ i. 5, 7.

It is therefore evident that the Christian theory of angels differed in no degree whatever from the Pagan theory of gods or demons; and that the Pagans themselves probably used the term angels as a synonym for the gods long before there were Christians to use it at all. But it is possible to go even farther, and to say that even Christian converts continued to speak of the gods in a manner proving how very superficial was the distinction between their belief and that of the Pagans, seeing that it did not always extend even to a difference in terminology. Tertullian speaks of the Roman emperor as next indeed to God, but as greater than the gods themselves.[1] The Christianity too of Clemens, who from a philosopher became a Christian and head of the catechetical school of Alexandria towards the end of the second century, has never been impeached; yet he often speaks of the gods as any Pagan might have spoken of them. He refers to the blessed abodes of the gods; he speaks of angels and gods as spectators of the contest between the true athlete and his passions; he declares all the host of angels and gods to be placed in subjection to the Son of God.[2] "Knowledge," he says, "leads to the endless and

[1] *Ad Scapulam*, 2: Sic omnibus major est (*i.e.* Imperator) dum solo vero Deo minor est; sic et ipsis diis major est dum et ipsi in potestate ejus.

[2] *Stromata*, vii. 2, 3: τούτῳ πᾶσα ὑποτέτακται στρατιὰ ἀγγέλων τε καὶ θεῶν.

perfect end, teaching us beforehand the future life we shall lead according to God and with gods," and such as, after purificatory punishment, are admitted to everlasting contemplation, "are called by the appellation of the gods, being destined to sit on thrones with the other gods that have been first put in their places by the Saviour."[1]

St. Augustine was as prominent a Christian as Clemens; but he also speaks of the "good gods who dwell in the holy and heavenly habitation, by whom we mean holy angels and rational creatures, whether thrones or dominations, or principalities or powers"; and again he says: "We must by no means seek, through the supposed mediation of demons, to enjoy the benevolence of the gods, or rather of the good angels."[2] So that Augustine and Clement were as much polytheists as Seneca or Plutarch; or rather, their monotheism must be taken with exactly the same reservations.

Therefore in the sense of angels subordinate to the Supreme God, the only sense of Pagan polytheism, the Christians did not deny a plurality of gods. In this alone they differed from the Pagans, that, whereas the latter regarded most of the demons as beneficent

---

[1] *Stromata*, vii. 10: θεοὶ τὴν προσηγορίαν κέκληνται οἱ σύνθρονοι τῶν ἄλλων θεῶν τῶν ὑπὸ τῷ Σωτῆρι πρώτων τεταγμένων γενησόμενοι.

[2] *City of God*, viii. 24, 25: Nullo modo igitur per daemonum medietatem ambiendum est ad benevolentiam deorum, vel potius bonorum angelorum.

beings, tender and loving towards mankind, they condemned all the Pagan Gods, demons or angels, as either bad or fallen spirits, and, without denying their real existence, maintained—as St. Augustine was so fond of maintaining—that they only interfered with men at all for the sensual pleasure of licking the blood from the altars. Against the bad angels or demons into which they thus resolved the gods of the Pagans, they set as good angels or gods the gods of the Jews. This is proved by reference to Origen, who, in regard to the expression in Psalm xcv. that God was Lord above all gods, explains these gods to mean, not those of the heathen, but the gods who are spoken of in Psalm lxxxii. as forming the assembly of gods, in the midst of whom God is there said to stand and judge.[1] He therefore distinguishes between real gods and nominal gods,— a distinction which Arnobius, the Christian controversialist, also recognises,[2] and which turns apparently merely on the nationality, Hebrew or Gentile, of the people whose Gods they were. The gods of the Jews or Christians were real; those of the Greeks and Romans only nominal.

In other words, Origen, in the sense of the identity between gods and angels, frankly recognised the polytheism of the ancient Jews, a polytheism which is plainly enough expressed in such passages as the

[1] *Against Celsus*, viii. 3.   [2] ii. 62.

following: Psalm lxxxvi. 8, "There is none like unto Thee among the gods, O Lord"; or Psalm cxxxvi. 2, "O give thanks unto the God of gods." And, irrespectively of these gods or angels, it is only to a monotheism in point of worship, not of belief, that the Jews can lay claim, their belief and trust in their own national God, Jehovah, never excluding their belief in, but only their worship of, the gods of other nations, as is shown by Exodus xv. 11, "Who is like unto thee, O Lord, among the gods?" or by Exodus, xviii. 11, where Jethro says, "Now I know that the Lord is greater than all gods."

In fact, a precisely similar religious development may be traced in Jewish history to that traceable in Greek, a gradual evolution of purer conceptions of the Deity starting from conceptions of the rudest anthropomorphism. The Christians reaped the advantage of all that generations of thinkers had done to purify men's ideas on theism, but of thinkers among whom the Hebrew prophets were certainly not more influential than the Pagan philosophers. Especially did they owe to the latter a clearer definition of the divine attributes than the Hebrews, with their greater indifference to logical precision, ever achieved. We owe them of course an infinite debt for their share in the liberation of the world from the enormous weight of absurd theology which in certain quarters of heathenism still held sway; but the

Christian polemic against the Pagan gods was only longer, not more effective, than the polemic of the Pagans themselves. There is nothing against them in Lactantius or Arnobius or Augustine or Tertullian that was not also in Plato or Cicero or Seneca or Varro; nor is it likely that the former would have ever succeeded in their work at all but for the efficiency with which the philosophers had done theirs. In later times, when the contest had become embittered between Christianity and Paganism, many Pagans would not so much as hear Cicero's *De Natura Deorum* read, and even wished the senate to destroy his writings, for the countenance they were held to give to the Christian hostility to the gods.[1] But this need not have been; for with a little more forbearance, a little more toleration for the traditions of ages on the part of the Christian reformers, the Pagan gods would have vanished from the earth more peaceably than they did; the absurd rites and superstitions would have died a natural death just as the oracles did; and if persecutions and martyrdoms attended their departure, it was because, unhappily, from a very early age, the propagation of Christianity passed out of the control of its more tolerant first teachers into that of men who, like Tertullian and Tatian, substituted intolerant contempt for calm reason, and who in their bigotry hesitated not to heap

[1] Arnobius, iii. 7.

on the most sacred convictions of their contemporaries the language of the bitterest insult and defiance.

It was not the spirit of real Christianity that prevailed over Paganism, but the spirit of extreme fanatics who claimed the name of Christians, without any true appreciation of its meaning.

CHAPTER II

PAGAN THEOLOGY

For several centuries before Christianity the brisk interchange of ideas between all the countries of the then known world produced what amounted to a system of International Philosophy or Religion, which, overriding all subordinate sects, prevailed from India to Gaul, and in which it is hopeless to trace or apportion the claims of the several nations to priority of conception. Whether the tradition is true or not that Pythagoras derived instruction from Egypt, Chaldaea, Persia, Gaul, and Iberia, in his objection to the taking of oaths, to the custom of prayers and sacrifices, to the slaughter of animals, as well as in his belief in the transmigration of souls, it is difficult not to believe, that through him, as perhaps also through Plato, the teaching of the great Buddha travelled at least as far as Greece and Italy. To what precise degree, if at all, the Greeks were influenced by Egypt and India, or the Jews were indebted to Persia and Assyria, we may never know; but it is beyond question that, at the beginning of the Christian era and for some time before, there was a great amalgamation of philosophical and religious ideas, uniting, as they have never been united since, India, Persia, Egypt, Greece, Italy, and probably France and Spain.

The belief in the overruling all-seeing Providence of God was among these universal ideas, and it is pleasing to remember that the Jew possessed it no more than the Greek or the Roman. Apuleius uses the phrase, Divine Providence, precisely as he might have done had he been a Christian.[1] The new religion added absolutely nothing new on the subject to the teaching we still find in Plato or Cicero; nor can we do better, if we would realise how very little speculation or controversy has varied on this problem within the last two thousand years, than trace in Seneca the presence of the very same reasonings, the very same doubts and difficulties, that still perplex the subject in modern times, and seem likely to perplex it for ever.

"What was for our good," says Seneca, "God, who is also our Father, placed ready to our hand."[2] "Whatever has been denied to us, it was impossible to give . . . we were and still are the favourite creatures of the immortal gods." It is better therefore for us, he urges, to contemplate and give

---

[1] *Golden Ass*, ix. 177: Divinae Providentiae fatalis dispositio.
[2] *Epist.* 110.

thanks for the many and great benefits we enjoy than to complain because in some respects we are inferior to other animals or have no knowledge of the future.[1]

Anticipating, however, modern science, Seneca places the laws of natural phenomena apart from the providential government of man. He protests against the folly of attributing to the gods such things as storms at sea, excessive rains, or long winters; and holds it a mistake to suppose that any of them occur from reference to ourselves: "We are not the cause of the return of summer and winter to the world; all such phenomena follow their own laws, and we esteem ourselves too highly if we deem ourselves worthy of the operation of such mighty occurrences."[2] Or again: "It is not by the anger of the gods that heaven and earth are shaken; such phenomena have their own causes, nor rage at any behest."[3] Man in short, though the favourite, is not the sole care of God. "How many bodies besides those we see in the heavens follow their secret courses unseen of mortal eyes, for God has not made all things for man."

But it is still more interesting to follow Seneca in his speculations on the moral government of the world. Why, for instance, did Providence place a man like

---

[1] *De Beneficiis*, ii. 29.   [2] *De Ira*, ii. 27.
[3] *Naturales Quaestiones*, vi. 3.

Caligula at the head of the civilised world? Seneca's suggestion is that such anomalies are allowed out of regard for the virtues of a man's ancestors or parents, or sometimes perhaps from consideration for the virtues of his posterity. "For the gods know beforehand the whole series of future events, and what we think sudden and unaccountable is to them foreseen and expected."[1] Why, again, on the theory of a Providence, do as many calamities befall the good as the bad? Seneca answers that in this way God tries the good man, hardens him, and prepares him for Himself. The shocks of adversity can no more change the mind of a brave man than all the rivers and waters can change the saltness of the sea. They are all trials. "Not what you bear, but how you bear it, is of importance." Towards good men God has the mind of a Father, and loves them in a strong manner, wishing them to gain strength by work, grief, and loss. Desiring them to rise to the highest pitch of excellence, He sends them a fortune which shall exercise their powers. A brave man struggling with misfortune is a spectacle worthy of God. And things that are called hard are for the good, first of all, of those to whom they happen, and then, of all men generally, the gods being more concerned with the general than the individual welfare. The good man may be called wretched, but he cannot be so. Exile,

[1] *De Beneficiis*, iv. 31.

or the loss of children, or the loss of husband and wife, may be beneficial, just as a surgical operation may be; and that was a good remark of Demetrius, that he never saw anything more unhappy than a man who had never suffered adversity. Were it not for bad fortune there would be no great samples of conduct; nor has human depravity yet fallen so low but that most men would rather be born to the destiny of a Regulus than to that of a Mecaenas. A man's greatness cannot be shown without opportunities for its display. To suffer is part of the glory of virtue. Those whom God loves He hardens and tries; and those whom He seems to favour and spare, He preserves without defence against future evils. No one is exempt; and the man who has long been happy will have his share. If called on to suffer, we should rejoice that God should have thought worthy to try in our own persons how much human nature can endure. As masters with their pupils, so the gods with good men : they require more labour from those of whom they have the highest hopes.

Also it is for the good of all that the best men should bear the brunt of the toilsome campaign of life. Wishing to show the falsity of the common distinction between good and evil things, God could not do so better than by letting so-called good things fall to the lot of the bad, and so-called evil things to that of the good. Labour is the portion of the best men; and in the great republic of life it is ever the good who toil and sacrifice themselves and are voluntarily sacrificed. One reason for resignation is that all is predestined: "Our destinies lead us, and the time of life that remains to each was settled at his natal hour. Cause hangs on cause; a long chain of events draws public and private affairs; and so we shall bear all with patience, for things do not, as we think, happen, but come. Your joys and griefs were long ago prefixed, and however various may seem the lives of individuals, the whole matter comes to this: perishable ourselves, we are the recipients of perishable gifts. Why then are we angry? why do we complain? It is for this we are prepared. Let Nature use the bodies that are hers as she will; but let ourselves, glad in every event, and brave, reflect that nothing that is really our own perishes." Moreover, God does not suffer any real evil to happen to the good. Things really evil he has removed from them, such as wickedness, crimes, evil thoughts, ambition, lust, or avarice; and good men suffer willingly the afflictions sent to them by God. They suffer in order to teach others to suffer. They are born as an example to men.[1]

And as to the objection that the ungrateful, as well as the good, share in the favours of Heaven, the answer is, that they only so share them, because it

[1] *De Providentia.*

was impossible for the benefits of sunshine and rain and the seasons to be apportioned according to goodness and badness. Also it was better to benefit even the bad for the sake of the good than to fail the good on account of the bad. As men have their share in the public corn, not as good or bad men, but simply as citizens, so as human beings, and not as good or bad men, do all share alike in the blessings of existence. God gave certain gifts to the whole human race without exception; the same wind that was favourable to the good could not also have been injurious to the bad, nor could falling showers have been forbidden to water the fields and crops of the wicked.[1]

In all this it will be seen that Seneca's belief did not differ in any essential respect from that which has ever been current since. Yet it was not merely Seneca's belief, but the common belief of his time, and especially of the Stoic philosophy from its very earliest days. This we know from the titles or fragments of the treatises of the earlier Stoics; and Epictetus but stated a commonplace when he argued that even such small things as the production of milk from grass, of cheese from milk, or of wool from skins, was enough to make a man perceive the providence of God. "Who made and devised these things?" he exclaims. "No one, you say! O

[1] *De Beneficiis*, iv. 28.

amazing shamelessness and stupidity!"[1] "Has the world no governor? How, if a city or family cannot exist the shortest time without a governor and guardian, shall so great and beautiful a system be administered with such order, and yet without a purpose and by chance?"[2] "Who made the sun, and the fruits of the earth, and the seasons, and the connection and fellowship of men with one another?"[3] "Is the sun able to illuminate so large a part of the all and to leave only without light so much as is occupied by the earth's shadow, and cannot He, who made the sun itself, a small part of Himself when compared with the whole, see all things?"[4]

Implicit trust in the goodness of Providence afforded the common consolation under bereavement to the Pagans, as it still does to Christians. Plutarch, writing to Apollonius to console him for the death of a son, suggests that the Deity, with a fatherly providence and out of tenderness to mankind, foreseeing the future, takes some of us purposely from the world by an untimely death; and urges that it would have been only according to human nature for the father to have died first, "but Providence hath other measures, and the supreme order that governs the world is very different."

As a rule, the providence that overruled humanity was held to be entrusted to the demons or angels

[1] *Discourses*, i. 16.   [2] *Ib.* ii. 14.   [3] *Ib.* iv. 1.   [4] *Ib.* i. 14.

who acted on earth as the guardians and overseers of human actions; and the guardian angel, who was set over each soul that was born into the world, was a commonly accepted article of pre-Christian belief. Sometimes it was thought of as a spirit apart from the soul, but more often as the soul itself, or even as conscience. Apuleius, for instance, speaks of the god which is each man's soul, and which, though immortal, is born with a man;[1] whilst Olympiodorus, following Plato, identifies the guardian angel with the conscience, the sinless part of our soul, the incorruptible judge and witness to the judges after death of the things done in the soul, and so the cause of salvation to us by always turning the soul to what is right, and suffering it not to fall under the dominion of sin. The Christian belief of the guardian angel accompanying the soul into the presence of its judge was simply the old belief as laid down in the *Phaedo* of Plato, that the demon or genius that attends a man in life leads him after death to the place of judgment.

To reconcile with the belief in Providence the existence of moral and physical evil in the world was one of the great problems of ancient, as it is still of modern, philosophy. There has been neither change nor advance in either the statement or the

---

[1] *De Deo Socratis*, 687: Is Deus qui est animus sui cuique, quamquam sit immortalis, cum homine gignitur.

solution of the problem. "Why did God," Cicero makes his sceptic argue, "if, as you Stoics will have it, He made all things for our sake, make so great a quantity of serpents and vipers? Why did he scatter over sea and land so many destructive things?"[1] No one ever stated more clearly all the evils incident to human life than did Maximus of Tyre, nor did any one ever protest more strongly against attributing to them a Divine causation. His explanation was just the same that is popular still; partly that the evils of individuals may really conduce to the good of the whole, partly that they are a natural consequence of human wickedness. The explanation of evil practically resolved itself into a denial of its existence. Nothing was really evil, argued the Stoics, that was according to Nature, and therefore death itself was no evil. Or else evil was but a means to a good end, and Chrysippus could see in so dreadful a calamity as the Trojan war an interposition on the part of the gods to check over-population: an argument which Plutarch justly and indignantly rejected as quite incompatible with the humane and beneficent character of the Divine nature.[2]

Perfect faith in the goodness of Providence, and perfect resignation to God's will, cast from some minds the idea of the necessity of prayer alto-

[1] *Acad. Quaest.* iv. 38. [2] *Contradictions of Stoics*, 32.

gether; and one of the most interesting dissertations of Maximus of Tyre gives us a good insight into the question of prayer, of its efficacy and rightful objects, as it presented itself to Pagan thought. That God could be influenced by prayer would, he contends, argue His changeability, an idea incompatible with the idea of Divine goodness. And further: "He that prays either is worthy of the things he prays for, or he is not. If he is, he will obtain them, even though he prays not; and if he is not, he will not obtain them, even though he prays. For neither does he that is worthy and neglects to pray become unworthy through the fact of not praying, nor does he that is unworthy but prays ·to obtain become worthy by the fact of praying; but, on the contrary, he that is worthy to obtain is so much the more worthy by not being importunate, whilst he that is unworthy adds to his unworthiness by his importunity. . . . . God therefore will neither give to those who pray, contrary to their deserts, nor refuse to those who pray not, according to their deserts."

And then again prayer is inconsistent with Providence; for the Providence of God either applies to the universe of things, and is indifferent to particulars, or else to particulars as well; in neither case is prayer necessary, for in the former it will be refused, if contrary to the good of the whole, whilst in the latter, to pray is to do as a sick man who should beg his doctor for some particular medicine or food, not resting assured that if it be good for him it will be given to him, though he ask not, but that if bad for him, not even though he ask.

Again, it is wrong to pray for wealth or victory or success in trade; "for God says: if thou askest for good things for a good object, and art worthy to ask for them, receive them. So thou hast no need of prayer, and shalt receive them, even though thou keepest silence. And if it be said that Socrates and Pythagoras and Plato used to pray, their prayer was not a petition for things that were wanting to them, but an intercourse and communing with the gods about the things they possessed, and an exercise of virtue. Socrates prayed the gods not for wealth nor power, but for a virtuous soul, a tranquil life, a blameless existence, a death of good hope (εὔελπιν θάνατον). But if a man shall pray for such things as a fair voyage from shore, or for plenty of fish from the sea, he will depart without obtaining the gifts for which he prayed."[1] Ask the gods, he says elsewhere, not about your ravaged fields, or pirates at sea, or your walls besieged, or your bodies destroyed, for these are trifles, and ephemeral; but ask about virtue, when your soul is injured, robbed, besieged, or diseased.[2]

[1] *Dissert.* xi.   [2] *Dissert.* xxviii.

The sum of all this is, that prayer should be for moral and spiritual, and not for temporal, blessings. We are constantly told that this was an exclusively Christian conception, and therefore some more evidence may be adduced to that wherewith Maximus of Tyre has already supplied us. Plutarch speaks of prayers as customary to the gods, not only for health, wealth, concord or peace, but for direction to the use of the best words and actions.[1] He mentions with approval such vows in prayers as to abstain from wine for a year and to serve God with temperance, or to be careful not to disregard truth even in jest; and he traced his own power of self-control to the habit he thus imposed on himself of avoiding anger on certain sacred days, a habit that in a few months' time rendered him much more patient of evil and more courteous in language and behaviour.[2] When the Roman consul, Telesinus, asked Apollonius of Tyana, the Pythagorean, what he prayed for at the altars, the philosopher replied, "That justice may prevail, the laws not be broken, that wise men may be poor, and the rest rich, but honestly"; and when he was further asked whether he thought that his prayer would be heeded, he answered, "Yes; for when I approach the altars, I include all in one prayer, 'Grant, O God, all that is good for me.'"[3] This prayer

[1] *Superstition*, iv. [2] *Cure of Anger*, xvi. [3] Philostratus, iv. 40.

he thought enough for all who came to the altar with a good conscience, in the presence of the all-knowing gods.[1] So Seneca bade Lucilius pray for a good conscience and good health of soul before asking for health of body; and, commending the precept of Athenodorus to ask nothing of God that could not be asked openly, he condemned the practice of some who dared to whisper most disgraceful prayers to the gods, and who told to God what they would not like a man to know. He finished his letter with words that no Christian writer has ever surpassed: "So live with men as if God saw you, so speak with God as if men heard you."[2] "That worship of the gods," says Cicero, "is the best and the most chaste, the holiest and the most religious, when we reverence them ever with purity and perfect innocence both of thought and word.[3]

Few traces remain of pre-Christian or Pagan prayer. The public prayers of the temple services of Rome or Athens are as little known to us as the prayers of the Chinese. In point of length and frequency they probably differed very little from what has since been customary. We find Marcus Aurelius bidding himself on all occasions to call on the gods, and not to trouble about the length of time so spent, for that even three hours of prayer

---

[1] Philostratus, *Life of Apol.* i. 11. [2] *Epist.* 10.
[3] *De Natura Deorum*, ii. 28.

would be enough; a fact which intimates that three hours was rather below than in excess of the time generally devoted to private prayer.

It would be more interesting to judge of the quality of the prayers; but for that the data fail, and we can only conjecture that, as with regard to their frequency and duration, so with regard to their subject-matter, their spirit, and their sentiments, the change effected by Christianity was less than we are apt to suppose. It is a distinct probability that, in the fusion that ultimately took place between Paganism and Christianity, many of the prayers that we still use passed with very little change from the religious services of Pagan to those of Christian Rome; for the inducement would have been irresistible to try to reconcile men to the new religion as often by the use of the old familiar words as by the use of the old familiar ceremonies.

But, to leave the ground of conjecture, we may fitly conclude this subject with a translation of the prayer to Zeus, with which Simplicius, the last of the philosophers, ended his commentary on Epictetus. If we may regard it as typical of pre-Christian prayer generally, we shall see that there cannot have been that lack of genuine piety of feeling which those who have nothing but black on their palettes for the Pagan world would fain have us believe. It runs as follows:—

"I beseech Thee, O Lord, the Father and Guide of our reason, to make us mindful of the noble origin Thou hast thought worthy to confer upon us; and to assist us to act as becomes free agents; that we may be cleansed from the irrational passions of the body and may subdue and govern the same, using them as instruments in a fitting manner; and to assist us to the right direction of the reason that is in us, and to its participation in what is real by the light of truth. And thirdly, I beseech Thee, my Saviour, entirely to remove the darkness from the eyes of our souls, in order that we may know aright, as Homer says, both God and man."

CHAPTER III

PAGAN RELIGION

NEXT to the fundamental unity of God, His perfect and absolute goodness was the most important principle dwelt upon by philosophical theology,—a principle not foreign, of course, to the higher religious conceptions of the ancient Jews, but a principle of such difficult reconcilement with many of their doctrines, as well as of those of the early Christian Church, as to have been one of the main grounds for which numbers from the very first deserted the Christian fold. Whatever doctrine conflicts with this first principle of the goodness of God, Philosophy asserted, as she still asserts, to be false; and the gross superstitions that have filled the world from the neglect of that plain and simple rule compel our admiration for the wisdom of Seneca, Epictetus, or Plutarch, who never tired of insisting on a right conception of God as the beginning and chief part of piety. "He worships God who knows Him" (*Deum colit qui novit*), said Seneca; and hence he deduced the vanity of lighting lamps on the Sabbath or paying morning devotions in the temples, and scorned the idea of the Deity standing in need of certain human services, on the ground that He could be in no need of servants who was Himself at the service of all men everywhere.[1] In reference to the worship of God, his words that "Love cannot be mingled with fear,"[2] correspond exactly with the Christian utterance, "Perfect love casteth out fear."

From this primary axiom of philosophical theology several consequences flowed of great importance in the religious sentiments of the Pagan world. First, a fervent feeling of love for God; secondly, a spirit of absolute but hopeful resignation to His will; and thirdly, the aspiration to imitate as far as possible His perfections. It is worth while to glance at each in turn, in order to understand aright the higher religious conceptions current among men who owed nothing to Jewish or Christian influences.

1. The conception of the all-pervading goodness of God is perhaps more apparent in Epictetus than in any other Pagan writer; certainly no other so clearly expressed man's duty of love and thankfulness for all the blessings of Providence. "For if we had understanding," he exclaims, "what else ought

---

[1] *Epist.* 95. [2] *Ib.* 47.

we to do publicly or privately than to sing hymns and give thanks to the Deity?" On every occasion we ought to sing a hymn, lauding the greatness of God; but since most of us are blind, "should there not be some one man to fulfil this office, and to sing, on behalf of all, the hymns to God? For what else can I, a lame old man, do than sing hymns to God? If I were a nightingale, I should act as a nightingale, and if a swan, as a swan; but since I am a rational being, it behoves me to praise God; this is my work; I do it, nor will I desert my post so long as I am allowed to keep it, and I exhort you to join in the same song."[1] It would be absurd to suppose that Epictetus was alone in the possession or the expression of such feelings; as large a proportion of the world probably possessed them then as possess or give utterance to them now.

2. From the love of God, flowing from the most perfect faith in His goodness, flowed as a necessary consequence a spirit of the most complete trust in His ordering of things, a spirit of the most implicit resignation to His will. This was the meaning of the old Pythagorean and Stoic precept, "Follow God," nor did the new Christian faith add anything to the sure guidance of life or to the consolation for its evils with which the recognition of this principle had for ages supplied pre-Christian society.

[1] *Discourses*, i. 16.

Of this let a few quotations from Seneca and Epictetus supply the proof.

"It is best," says Seneca, "to suffer what you cannot amend, and to follow God, the Author of all things, without murmuring; he is a bad soldier who groans as he follows his general."[1] "What is the principal thing? To be able to bear adversity with a cheerful mind; so to bear whatever happens as if you wished it to happen, for you ought to have wished it to happen, had you known that all things happen by the decree of God; to weep, to lament, to groan, is to rebel."[2] "A good man, being of the highest piety towards the gods, will bear with equanimity whatever happens to him, knowing that it happened by the Divine law from which all things flow."[3] "In all circumstances which seem opposed to me and hard, I am constituted in this wise: I do not merely obey God, but I yield assent to Him. I follow Him from my heart, not from necessity. Nothing shall ever happen to me which I will take sadly or with a bad face."[4]

This was the faith, the common sentiment of thousands, in whatever school of philosophy they were reared, in days when philosophy was practically identical with religion, and supplied men no less with a high standard of moral action than with

[1] *Epist.* 17. [2] Prolegomena to *Naturales Quaestiones*.
[3] *Epist.* 76. [4] *Ib.* 96.

support for the present and hope for the future life; when philosophy sent its missionaries to all parts of the world, to promote virtue and oppose vice, even, if need were, at the peril of their lives,—missionaries like Apollonius, Diogenes, Dion Chrysostom; and when philosophers, instead of confessors, lived in kings' and nobles' houses, to counsel them in life and to educate their children. Epictetus, on the duty of merging the human will in the Divine, will bear comparison with the author of the *Imitatio Christi* or with any other Christian writer. And yet we only have the faint reflection of his actual teaching, only notes worked up from his lectures by Arrian, the historian, who attended them!

"Dare to look up to God and say: Do with me henceforth as Thou wilt. I am of one mind with Thee. I am Thine. I decline nothing that seems good to Thee. Lead me whither Thou wilt. Clothe me as Thou wilt. Wilt Thou that I hold office or live a private life, remain at home or go into exile, be poor or rich, I will defend Thy purpose with me in respect of all these."[1]

In the same spirit he only professes himself as desirous, when disease or death shall overtake him, of being able thus to address God: "Have I transgressed Thy commandments? Have I used amiss the means Thou gavest me? . . . Have I ever

[1] *Discourses*, ii. 16.

blamed Thee? Have I ever found fault with Thy government? I have been ill, because it was Thy will, and so have others, but I willingly. At Thy will I became poor, but cheerfully. If I never held office, it was that Thou didst not will it, and so I never desired it. Didst Thou ever behold me the sadder on this account? Have I ever approached Thee with a sad countenance,—I ready to follow Thine orders and signals? And now dost Thou wish me to depart from Thine assembly? I depart, giving Thee all thanks that Thou hast thought me worthy to take part in Thy festival, to behold Thy works, and to appreciate Thy government."[1]

Elsewhere he expresses the hope that death may find him engaged in some work of human interest, something beneficent, of public utility, and noble; but that otherwise he may be found engaged in a work that nothing can hinder, the work of self-improvement ($\dot{\epsilon}\mu\alpha\upsilon\tau\grave{o}\nu$ $\dot{\epsilon}\pi\alpha\nu o\rho\theta\hat{\omega}\nu$). Then would he be content to stretch forth his hands to God and say: "The means that Thou gavest me to understand Thy government I have not neglected. I for my part have not dishonoured Thee. . . . Have I ever blamed Thee? Have I ever been ill-pleased with anything that has happened or wished it to be otherwise? . . . That Thou hast brought me into life I thank Thee, and for what Thou hast given. I am

[1] *Discourses*, iii. 5.

content to have enjoyed for so long the things that were Thine. Receive them back again, and dispose of them where Thou pleasest. For Thine they all were. It was Thou who gavest them to me. Is it not enough to depart in such a spirit, and what life is better and more becoming than one so ordered, or what close of life more happy?"[1]

Epictetus therefore would have men talk, not of losing things, but of restoring them. "Is your child dead? It has been restored. Is your wife dead? She has been restored."[2] Man's freedom and happiness depend on his looking to God in all things, small or great, and in submitting his own will unconditionally to that of the Deity. Epictetus professes himself ready to follow God's will, even to death upon the rack;[3] and his ideal of the perfect Stoic is of a man ever desirous to be of the same mind with God, and of assenting submission to His decrees.

This idea of resignation is impressed on almost every page of Epictetus. It is the dominant spirit of all that remains of his life and teaching, as it is also of the *Meditations* of Marcus Aurelius, who set himself for the guiding principle of his life the precept, "Love mankind. Follow God."[4] On every occasion the Emperor would have a man reflect, This comes from God.[5] Such is his faith in the wisdom and

[1] *Discourses*, iv. 10.   [2] *Encheiridion*, ii.   [3] *Discourses*, iv. 1.
   [4] vii. 31.   [5] *Ib.* iii. 11.

benevolence with which things have been arranged for mankind, that he is content to leave the question unsolved whether good men who have led pious and religious lives in constant communion with the Divinity will be extinguished by death, in perfect trust that in whichever way it is destined to be, it has been ordered by the higher powers for the best.[1]

3. "Would you propitiate the gods?" exclaims Seneca. "Then be like them. He worships them enough who imitates them."[2] And this had been one of the commonplaces of philosophy from at least the time of Plato, who said, "He who would be dear to God must be like Him and such as He is."[3] It is a fine passage which Augustine quotes from Porphyry, who wrote a long but lost work against the Christians: "God being the Father of all, is in need of nothing; but for us it is good to adore Him by means of Justice, Chastity, and other virtues, and thus to make life itself a prayer to Him by inquiring into and imitating His nature. For inquiry purifies, and imitation deifies us, by moving us nearer to Him."[4]

Nothing perhaps more completely shows the falsity of the common assertion that the religious ideas of Paganism left men's lives and morals uninfluenced and unelevated than this idea of the human endeavour to imitate the Divine nature. Such an imitation was

---

[1] *Meditations*, xii. 5. [2] *Epist.* 95.
[3] *Laws*, iv. 716; *Theaetetus*, 133. [4] *City of God*, xix. 23.

only possible, said Seneca, by the possession of an upright, good, and great soul, which was nothing else than God resident in a human body. "By the attainment of perfect virtue, which is the chief good, you begin to be the companion of the gods, and not their suppliant. . . . The way is safe and pleasant, and one for which Nature has equipped you. If you but hold fast to what she has given you, you will rise equal to God."[1] To raise a man to an equality with God was therefore the promise of philosophy;[2] and philosophy he declared to be inseparable from religion, justice, piety, and all other virtues; philosophy that taught men to worship the gods and to love mankind (*colere divina, humana diligere*).[3]

Perfect mental happiness was the sign and consequence of the attainment of this state. "If you are never sad, and no hope perturbs your soul with future anxiety, if by day and night the tenor of your mind is equable, upright, self-satisfied, you have attained the sum of human felicity."[4]

In all this what is admirable is the proud reliance on human nature and the strong belief in its high capacities for virtue; a reliance and belief which must not only have served of themselves as powerful incentives to good, but have acted also as powerful safeguards against great moral debasement. Whether the keen sense of personal and general sinfulness,

[1] *Epist.* 31.   [2] *Ib.* 48.   [3] *Ib.* 90.   [4] *Ib.* 59.

which came into the world with the Oriental religions, ever proved as efficient, may well be doubted; the habit of dwelling on the higher possible attainments of our nature would seem to have a better tendency than that of always harping on its lower depths. The Stoic doctrine, that the human soul or reason was a part of, or emanation from, the Divinity, led certainly to as high conceptions of the moral and spiritual elevation, attainable by assiduous discipline and effort, as was ever promoted by the Hebrew doctrine of the fallen and corrupt nature of humanity. But at all events between the two points of view, whichever we prefer, there was a perfect abyss, as the following passages from Seneca will show.

"You ask what constitutes a wise man. The same as constitutes God, for you must allow the former to possess something divine, heavenly, and magnificent. . . . You ask, What is the locality of the sovereign good? The soul; which, unless it is pure and holy, cannot receive God." [1]

"Between good men and the gods there is a friendship founded on virtue. Friendship, do I say? nay, rather an intimacy and likeness, for a good man only differs in point of time from God, whose disciple he is, and imitator, and also His real offspring." [2]

"In what does Jupiter surpass a good man? In the longer duration of his goodness; a wise man does

[1] *Epist.* 87.   [2] *De Providentia*, 1.

not think less of himself because his virtues are included in a shorter space of time. As of two wise men he that dies the oldest is not happier than the other, whose virtue is ended within a few years, so God does not surpass a wise man in felicity, albeit he does in length of time. The virtue is not greater in itself which is longer in time. . . . We should follow Sextius, who points the road to heaven through frugality, temperance, and fortitude. The gods are not fastidious or jealous; they admit and stretch out their hands to those who ascend to them. Do you wonder that a man should go to the gods? It is God who comes to men, nay, rather comes into men, for there is no good mind without God."[1]

There are few writers who have not held up to scorn the apparent arrogance of these words. Yet the idea of the innate divinity of man flowed necessarily from that theory of the soul which regarded it as originally emanating from God, and as ultimately destined to return to its source. It was in this sense that men were accustomed to think and speak of themselves as the sons of God. Epictetus calls man a portion separated from the Deity, a portion of Him.[2] "Why," he asks, "should not a man who has observed the government of the world, and the generation of all beings on the earth from God, call himself a citizen of the world and a son of God;

[1] *Epist.* 73.   [2] *Discourses*, ii. 8.

and if kinship with Caesar or any other great Roman enables us to live without fear, shall not the fact of God being our Maker and Father and Guardian release us from sorrows and anxiety?"[1] "Zeus has set me free," he exclaims; "do you think He intended His own Son to be enslaved?"[2] He argues that a man who realised the doctrine that we are all sprung from God would have no mean or ignoble thoughts about himself, and he makes the consideration a constant appeal to playing a noble and worthy part in life.

This, then, explains Seneca's language when he speaks of the truly good man equalling the gods, and, ever mindful of his origin, raising himself up to them. There can be nothing wrong, he urges, in a man's endeavour to ascend to the place whence he originally descended; and something divine may assuredly be held to exist in a man who is part of God. "For this whole in which we are contained is both one and is God; and we are His associates and members." "And as our body is erect and looks heavenwards, so our soul is capable of infinite expansion, and has been so formed by nature as to have the same wishes as the gods."[3]

In the same sense he writes: "We should so live as if we lived in the public gaze, and so think as if some one could inspect our inmost heart; and so

---

[1] *Discourses*, i. 9.   [2] *Ib*. i. 19.   [3] *Epist*. 92.

some one can, for what is the use of anything being concealed from man, when nothing is closed to God? He is present in our souls, and enters into our inmost thoughts. Enters, do I say, as if He were ever absent from them."[1] Or when again he tells Lucilius that there is no need to raise his hands in prayer to heaven, nor to beg the sacristan to admit him to the ears of the idol in order to be better heard, it is for the reason that "God is near you, is with you, is within you. Yes, a holy spirit resides within us, who watches our good and evil actions and also watches over us."[2]

It is necessary here to quote some parallel passages from Epictetus, which will still further serve as an answer to the common denial of the existence of any religious feeling in Pagan antiquity. "If you always remember that whatever you are doing in soul or body God stands by as an inspector, you will never err in all your prayers or acts, but you will have God dwelling with you."[3] Zeus "has placed by every man a demon or guardian who never sleeps nor is deceived. . . . When then you have shut the doors and made darkness within, never say you are alone, for you are not, but God is within, and your demon, and what need have they of light to see what you are doing?"[4] "The philosophers say that

[1] *Epist.* 83. [2] *Ib.* 41. [3] Fragment 120.
[4] *Discourses*, i. 14.

we ought first to learn that there is a God and that He provides for all things; and that it is impossible to conceal from Him our acts, or even our intentions and thoughts."¹ "When you are going to see any great person, remember that another also from above sees what is going on, and that you ought to please Him rather than the other."² "You are carrying a God with you, and you know it not. Do you think I mean some god of silver or gold, and external? You carry Him within yourself, and you do not perceive that it is Him you pollute by impure thoughts and dirty deeds. And if an image of God were present, you would not dare to do any of the things which you are doing; but when God Himself is present within and sees all and hears all, you are not ashamed of thinking such things and doing such things, ignorant as you are of your own nature and subject to the anger of God."³ "Live with the gods," says Aurelius, "and He does live with them who constantly shows them that His own soul is satisfied with what is assigned to Him, and that it does all that the demon wishes, which Zeus hath given to every man for his guardian and guide, a portion of Himself: and this is every man's understanding and reason."⁴

It is moreover noteworthy that Seneca's language about the possible equality of man with God is

¹ *Discourses*, ii. 14.   ² *Ib.* i. 30.   ³ *Ib.* ii. 8.   ⁴ v. 27.

equalled not only by other Pagan writers, but at least by two of the most philosophic of the Christian Fathers. Cicero has a fine passage in his *Republic*: "So consider it, that it is not thou who art mortal, but only this body of thine.... The soul of each man constitutes himself, not that figure which can be shown by the finger. Know, therefore, that thou art a god, since he is a god who flourishes, who feels, who remembers, who uses foresight, who rules and governs that body over which it is set, just as that Supreme God rules and moves this world."[1] Elsewhere he speaks of piety, justice, and the other virtues as constituting a happy life, "equal and similar to that of the gods, yielding in nothing to the celestials save in immortality."[2]

But it is more surprising to find similar language in St. Clement, Lactantius, and Tertullian. Lactantius speaks of a man who masters his passion as becoming the equal of God (*Hic erit consimilis Deo, qui virtutem · Dei cepit.*)[3] Clement declares that the man who leads his life on the true Gnostic principles is worthy to be called the Lord's brother, and at the same time His friend and son;[4] and in another place, after describing the virtues of the perfect Gnostic in language that throughout closely resembles the Stoics' descriptions of their ideal wise man, he concludes:

---

[1] vi. 17.   [2] *De Natura Deorum*, ii. 61.   [3] vi. 23.
[4] *Stromata*, iii. 10.

"In this way it is possible for the Gnostic already to have become God."[1] Tertullian, in praise of fasting, actually goes so far as to say that it makes God tent-fellow with man, peer in truth with peer.[2]

The principle of striving to imitate the Divine perfection was applied by the philosophers to every detail of moral action. From the nature of God, and the duty of man to strive to imitate it, Epictetus deduces the subordinate duty of being faithful, beneficent, and magnanimous in every word and act of life.[3] And Plutarch says: "There is no greater benefit men can enjoy from God than by the imitation and pursuit of His perfections and sanctity to be excited to the study of virtue"; whence he urges it as one reason for the slowness of God to punish, that men, imitating His mercy and forbearance, may be slower to take revenge on their fellows, nor hasten to inflict chastisement upon them[4]

A portion of a letter by Porphyry, the Neo-Platonist, to Marcella, his wife, may fitly close this part of the subject. "The best honour thou canst pay to God is to make thy soul resemble God; and

---

[1] *Stromata,* iv. 23, τούτῳ δυνατὸν τῷ τρόπῳ τὸν γνωστικὸν ἤδη γενέσθαι θεόν.

[2] *On Fasting,* 6. Tanta est circumscripti victus praerogativa ut Deum praestet homini contubernalem, parem revera pari. Si enim Deus aeternus non esuriet, ut testatur per Esaiam, hoc erit tempus quo homo Deo adaequetur cum sine pabulo vivet.

[3] *Discourses,* ii. 14.   [4] *Slowness of God to Punish,* 5.

this resemblance will be possible only by virtue, for virtue alone draws the soul upwards towards its like. And nothing else is accounted great with God than virtue, but God is greater than virtue, and strengthens the well-doer, but a bad spirit is a guide to bad deeds. A bad soul therefore flees from God and will not admit there is a providence of God, and utterly rejects the Divine law which punishes every wicked man. But the soul of a wise man conforms itself to God, always looks to God, is always with God. God cares and provides for the wise man, and therefore the wise man is blessed, because he is under God's protection. It is not the utterances of the wise man that God values, but his works, for the wise man, even though silent, honours God, whilst the illiterate man, even when he prays and sacrifices, profanes the Divinity. The wise man therefore alone is a priest, alone beloved of God, alone knows how to pray. He who practises wisdom practises the knowledge of God, not by always praying and sacrificing, but by showing by works his piety towards God. For one makes himself pleasing to God, not by behaving according to the opinions of man or the empty phrases of sophists, but a man makes himself pleasing to God and deifies himself by assimilating his own soul to the Being who enjoys an incorruptible beatitude. A man makes himself pleasing or displeasing to God, nor does he suffer evil at the hands of God. For he is not so impious who does not worship the statues of the gods, as he who attaches to God the opinions of the multitude. But do thou be persuaded that we cannot form an high enough idea of God, of His beatitude and incorruptibility. . . . And it is not by certain rites nor opinions that we rightly worship God. God is not moved either by tears or supplications; sacrifices do not honour him, nor are a multitude of offerings an ornament to Him, but the soul that is well governed and full of the Divine spirit enters into union with God, for like must join with like. And the sacrifices of the senseless are food for fire, and their offerings are a prey for the sacrilegious. But do thou, as I have said, make of thine own mind the temple of God; let it be prepared and adorned as a fitting receptacle for Him."

From the same letter some detached sentences will tend still further to support the inference, sought to be enforced, of the fundamental identity between the higher Christian religious sentiment and that of the pre-Christian or extra-Christian world. They are the more interesting as coming from an avowed enemy of Christianity and a writer of a voluminous work against it, all copies of which were burnt by the Christians in the reign of Theodosius. "Wherever forgetfulness of God creeps in, there the bad spirit (ὁ κακὸς δαίμων) must dwell. For the soul is the habitation of either gods or demons." "Of every action and every deed and word let God be present as observer and overseer, and of all our good deeds let us deem God the cause." "The labour which other people undergo for the sake of the body, so much does the wise man and God-loving undertake for the benefit of his soul." "Great training is required for the government of the body; and often for this purpose are certain members cut off. Be thou ready for the salvation of thy soul to cut off thy whole body." "Let these four principles above all be held firmly as elementary concerning God: faith, truth, love, hope. For it behoves us to believe that the only salvation is conversion to God; to be zealous above all things to have a right knowledge of Him; knowing Him, to love Him; and loving Him, to cherish good hopes about life."[1]

The foregoing evidence proves conclusively that in love and thankfulness to God for His goodness, in trustful resignation to His providence and will, in a moral and spiritual endeavour to bring human life into conformity with His perfections, the Pagan world, as represented by its higher teachers, had no lesson to learn of the Christian missionaries, nor any reason for transferring its allegiance from the religion inculcated by Philosophy. A few more extracts from

[1] For Porphyry's letter to Marcella see Orelli's *Opuscula*, i. 282-314.

Epictetus will minimise yet more the difference between the rival spiritual forces. Speaking of the struggle with temptation, he says: "Great is the combat, divine the work; it is for kingship, freedom, happiness, tranquillity. Remember God; call on Him as a helper and protector, as men at sea call on the Dioscuri."[1] "Desire to be in purity with your own pure self and with God."[2] "Wish nothing else but what God wishes."[3] "From your mind cast out ... sadness, fear, desire, envy, malice, avarice, effeminacy, intemperance. But it is only possible to cast them out by looking to God, by fervent attachment to Him, by devotion to His commands."[4] "Let your talk of God be renewed every day rather than your food."[5] "Think of God more frequently than you breathe."[6]

And then we must remember that all this is but from the merest surface of Pagan literature, and that the secrets of its real depths rest with the flames that destroyed the famous library at Alexandria, or with the fires that raged against Pagan literature during and probably long after the Christian persecution under Theodosius, or with the monks who scraped the old parchment manuscripts of the Pagans in order to cover them with their own legends. To judge of the influence and quality of pre-Christian

---

[1] *Discourses*, ii. 18. [2] *Ib.* ii. 18. [3] *Ib.* ii. 17.
[4] *Ib.* ii. 16. [5] Fragment 118. [6] *Ib.* 119.

religion we are reduced to an amount of published remains, which, compared with the books of the religion that finally prevailed, is suspiciously insignificant. To obtain any idea of the real religious feeling of antiquity, we are forced to gather it as best we may from moral or philosophical treatises, or from the poets, or from the fragments scattered through the pages of the Christian Fathers. We catch glimpses of it in Plato, or in the Neo-Platonists like Porphyry, Plotinus, or Jamblicus; albeit obscured in all the latter by their metaphysical speculations. We find more of it in the remains of Epictetus or Seneca—the late representatives of that Stoic school to whose philosophy the civilised world and afterwards the Christian world was so largely indebted for its higher moral and religious ideas. Yet how little, after all, remains of that philosophy! Of Zeno, its founder, the titles of some of his works; of the seven hundred and five treatises of Chrysippus, nothing but their titles or fragments; of Cleanthes, only that noble hymn to Zeus which rises to the highest level of the Hebrew Psalmists. All we know, from fragments or from allusions to the titles of their works, is that a large part of their writings, in other words their philosophy, was what we should now call religious, inculcating those duties towards God and mankind which man owed by virtue of his relationship to God. Even of the lectures of Epictetus, whereof we get a faint reflection of the original from the second-hand reproduction of Arrian, only four books have been preserved out of eight: whilst of Seneca, the titles of his lost works seem to show that we only possess a fraction of his total productions; and of him, as of Marcus Aurelius, it may be said, that his noblest thoughts, in his letters to Lucilius, were in the nature of private confidences, and not written with a view to publication at all. But enough remains to reveal the existence, even in the worst days of the Roman Empire, of a spiritual and religious life which it has suited most historians purposely to ignore, in order to account, by the theory of the religious destitution of Paganism, for the rapid progress of Christianity.

It is so much the custom to speak of Seneca and Epictetus as Stoics, that we are apt to overlook the fact that, in the sense of adopting the best doctrines of all philosophical schools alike, they have as much right as Cicero to be called Eclectics. The best ideas of Plato, Pythagoras, and Epicurus mingle in their teaching; and Seneca, who expressly disclaims any rigid adherence to a particular philosophical sect, quotes no other writer with more approval or more frequency than Epicurus. This Eclectic philosophy was the great triumph of Pagan thought; and the position it held, and the influence it had, may well be illustrated by a remark of Clement, the most liberal of the Christian Fathers, who claimed the inspiration of God as much for Greek philosophy as for the two Testaments, and who protested against the fear of it felt by his co-religionists as no better than that of children for ghosts: "By philosophy I do not mean the Stoic, or the Platonic, or the Epicurean, or the Aristotelian; but whatever has been finely said by each of these sects, teaching righteousness with pious knowledge, this eclectic whole I call philosophy."[1] Origen not only bears witness to the immense benefits conferred by philosophy, but admits that but for it Christianity would never have prevailed: "How was it possible for the Gospel doctrine of peace, not allowing us even to take vengeance on our enemies, to have prevailed in the world, unless at the advent of Jesus a milder spirit had been introduced?"[2] Justin Martyr did not scruple to count among the elect of God philosophers like Socrates, Heraclitus, or Musonius; and this more liberal attitude of Christianity towards the Pagan philosophy which had prepared the way for it was one of the marked characteristics of the earlier Church, as compared with the religious antipathy towards classical literature which reached its climax with Jerome, and which the Catholic Church has displayed from his day to our own.

After the mental nightmare, which with the triumph of Catholicism brooded over the world for

[1] *Stromata*, i. 7.   [2] *Against Celsus*, ii. 30.

some thousand years, the classical spirit of Hellenism began again to reassert itself. With the Swiss more than with the German Reformation, with Zwingli rather than with Luther, Greek thought again came into competition with Hebrew, colouring, enlarging, and ennobling Christianity. Sacred literature, rightly so called, included, according to Zwingli, Greek and Latin, as well as Hebrew writers. In a treatise on Providence he appealed in the same sentence to Plato and Seneca as of equal authority with Moses and St. Paul. He held that if the Pagan philosophers dared not profess a monotheistic belief, they nevertheless possessed it; and, as a corollary of the fundamental identity between profane and sacred literature, he openly taught in church that as many samples of noble lives might be found in profane as in Hebrew history. Socrates and Seneca, he boldly affirmed, "though they were ignorant of religion in the strict or sacramental sense of the word, yet in reality were more religious and holy than all the Dominicans and Franciscans that ever lived." To Francis I. of France he held out the hope of the enjoyment after death of the society of all the good and wise men who had ever been since the world began, not only of the Biblical celebrities, but of Theseus, Socrates, Aristides, Antigonus, Numa, Camillus, the Catos, the Scipios, and others. "No good man has ever been," he concluded; "no holy mind or faithful soul shall ever be, from the very beginning of the world to its close, whom you shall not see there in the company of God."

The slightest knowledge of the history of Christian thought will convince its possessor of the immeasurable advance over most of his predecessors, contemporaries, or successors, which was involved in these ideas of Zwingli. Not only was it the orthodox view handed down from Eusebius and Clement that all the higher ideas of the Greeks were, for no other reason than a certain distant similarity and posteriority in point of time, direct plagiarisms from Moses and the prophets, but also that all men, whatever their virtue, who lived before Christ, were condemned hopelessly to the punishment of everlasting flames for their share in the sin of Adam, and for their inevitable ignorance of the means of salvation from it! Zwingli's ideas were accordingly as distasteful to Luther and most of the Protestant theologians as they were to the Catholics; and they proved the greatest stumbling-block in the way of his success as a teacher. Now, of course, they are so commonly held that it is a source of wonder that there should have ever been a time when they were regarded as dangerous or heretical. It is to Zwingli and to the Broad Church school, descended from him, that we owe this progress of thought; and if this chapter should help still further to promote that progress, to convince us of the real Hellenic origin of our higher Christian religious ideas, and therefore to turn us from an exclusive study of Persianised Hebrew conceptions to the study of the pure and simple thoughts of Greek philosophy, it will not have been written in vain.

CHAPTER IV

PAGAN SUPERSTITION

It is difficult to judge how far the open scepticism of men like Cicero or Varro represented a general revulsion in Roman society from the earlier polytheistic religion. Our own experience should suffice to show how little correspondence there may be between the wide spread of scepticism over a society and its deep penetration; and inscriptions from all parts of the world seem to indicate that the people of the Roman Empire were as little disturbed by the intellectual commotion above them as are the depths of the sea by the winds upon its surface. The ridicule of Lucian would have been unmeaning had it not pointed to the extreme vitality or to the renewed vigour of the worst superstitions of the ancient creed.

Probably the never-ending conflict between scepticism and superstition served in those days as in our own to give strength and prominence to extremes in either direction; and Apuleius doubtless gave a fair picture of his contemporaries when he wrote the following: "The profane crowd of people, unskilled in philosophy, destitute of holiness, wanting in true reason, without religion, incapable of truth, most scrupulous in its religious worship, neglects the gods with the most insolent contempt; part of them superstitious, part contemptuous, either full of fear or full of pride. All these gods very many worship, though not aright, but all ignorantly fear them, and a few impiously deny them altogether."[1]

The difference between the religious and the superstitious man was happily touched by Maximus of Tyre, when he spoke of the former as the friend, and of the latter as the flatterer, of God. Over against the atheists who overlooked the gods, Plutarch set the superstitious who misunderstood them, wilfully mistaking their benign affection and providence for tyranny and cruelty, and refusing to listen to philosophers or statesmen who declared them to be good and beneficent; and he wondered at people who, whilst they condemned the atheists for impiety, acquitted the superstitious. "What!" he exclaims indignantly, "is he who holds that there is no God guilty of impiety, and is not he much more so who describes Him as the superstitious do?" Would not he himself prefer that people should deny the exist-

[1] *De Deo Socratis*, 668.

ence of Plutarch altogether than describe him as fickle, vindictive, and inhumane, as so many pictured the Deity?[1]

The superstitious element in Pagan life tended ever to prevail over the sceptical. The rapidity with which all religious innovations, especially from the East, spread over the Roman dominion, in spite of all legal opposition or persecution, proves the receptivity that then possessed the civilised world for new forms of worship. The worship, for instance, of Egyptian deities, like Isis, made its way in defiance of the Roman senate. Soon after the second Punic war there was a decree for the destruction of the temples of Isis and Serapis, and we hear of the consul Aemilius Paulus taking axe in hand against them when no workman dared to touch the sacred buildings.[2] Even the first temple publicly dedicated to Isis in 43 B.C. was destroyed by Tiberius, and the priests punished; but all persecution was in vain, for not only did the Isis religion speedily possess itself of the Imperial throne in the persons of Otho, Domitian, Commodus, Caracalla, and Alexander Severus, but inscriptions prove the new faith to have spread all over the Empire —to Spain, France, Switzerland, Germany, and even to England. The priests with their white linen dresses and bald-shaven heads, the clapping of the sistrum, the baptism with the Nile water, and the pageantry

[1] *Superstition*, 6, 10.   [2] Valerius Maximus, i. 2, 3.

of processions, so graphically painted by Apuleius, all point to a religion admirably calculated to spread among the multitude; but every part of the ceremonial, absurd as it may seem to us, had a clear symbolical meaning, and it is certain that the central idea of the worship of Isis and Osiris was the achievement of a holier life by means of atonement, fasting, and abstinences of all sorts, and the attainment of a purer life hereafter by withdrawal from the delights of this. "If by sedulous worship," Apuleius makes Isis say to Lucius in his famous story, "and by the services of religion and by constant chastity thou shalt promote my worship, thou shalt know that it rests with me alone to prolong thy life beyond the bounds accorded to it by Fate."[1] And the priest also say to Lucius: "The gates of Hell and the control of salvation are in the hands of the goddess, and her rites are celebrated in imitation of a voluntary death and difficult recovery; so that, as it were at the close of life and at the very limit of the enjoyment of light, those to whom the great mysteries of religion can be safely entrusted the goddess is wont to choose, and to restore them, born again in some way by her providence, to run the course of a new salvation."[2]

Against the inroad of every conceivable phase of

---

[1] *Golden Ass*, xii. 241.
[2] *Ib.* xi. 253. The word *renatos* = "born again" is remarkable in this passage.

Oriental religion the educated classes struggled in vain. The Greek mysteries of Eleusis, the Cappadocian worship of Bellona, the Phrygian worship of Cybele, or the Persian Mithra-worship, brooked no opposition. Persecution proved no less futile against them than it proved afterwards against Christianity. In the year 176 B.C. as many as 7000 persons were found guilty of taking part in the secret worship of Bacchus, and of these as many as half were killed.[1] In the reign of Tiberius no fewer than 4000 freedmen were exiled to Sardinia, to fight the brigands there, for participation in the Egyptian and Jewish religions, and probably the number was larger of those who for the same offence were forced to leave Italy or to give up their rites by a certain day.[2] Asceticism in its many forms had become the order of the day long before Christianity gave a fresh impetus in the same direction. Clement speaks of the idol-worshippers as refraining from food and observing a strict chastity.[3] Seneca describes people as spending whole days seated or standing before the idols, and sacrificing or throwing money to them.[4] He complains above all of the universal prevalence of Jewish customs, and deplores the loss of a seventh part of life involved in the observance of the Jewish Sabbath.[5]

[1] Livy, xxix. 8.   [2] Tacitus, *Annals*, ii. 85.
[3] *Stromata*, iii. 6 : Ii qui colunt idola a cibis et venere abstinent.
[4] Lactantius, *Divine Institutes*.
[5] Augustine, *City of God*, vi. 11.

This seems to justify Josephus, who declares that no Greek nor barbarian nation or town was so barbarous as not to observe the day of rest, nor to light lamps in God's honour and observe the Jewish fasts and abstinences.[1] The assurance indeed of Clement that the seventh day was regarded as sacred by the Greeks no less than by the Jews, is not borne out by his quotations from Homer, Hesiod, Callimachus, and the *Elegies* of Solon;[2] but Tertullian's allusion to the Romans as choosing the day of the Sun for rest, for banqueting, and for abstinence from the bath till the evening,[3] seems to indicate a wide observance of the Sabbath previous to the establishment of Christianity.

With keen and just contempt Seneca describes the persons who, to propitiate the gods, cut their arms or mutilated themselves, as if gods who required such services deserved to be worshipped at all; or who killed themselves in the temples, making their wounds and blood their supplication ; and who did or suffered things so unworthy of free men and so unlike rational beings that no one would have doubted their insanity but for their constituting a crowd instead of a minority.[4]

Tertullian admits in fact that the heathen observed every form of humiliation ($\tau\alpha\pi\epsilon\iota\nu o\phi\rho o\nu\eta\sigma\iota\varsigma$) that was more in keeping with Christianity : barefooted proces-

[1] *Contra Apion*, ii. 39.　[2] *Stromata*, v. 14.
[3] *Ad Nationes*, i. 13.　[4] Augustine, *City of God*, vi. 11.

sions were publicly proclaimed in time of drought; in some places it was an annual custom to go in sackcloth and ashes in supplication to the idols, and to keep all baths and shops closed till three in the afternoon.[1]

The success and spread of these superstitions, in spite of ridicule or persecution, prove that, all evidences of the faithless state of the early Roman Empire notwithstanding, the real condition was one of extreme religious fermentation, when every new form of faith or ritual met with prompt attention and acceptance.

With all these new religions, and especially with the religious mysteries, there was of course abundant imposture, knavery, and immorality; and the evidence on this point of Clement or Augustine adds nothing essential to the evidence of the Pagan writers themselves. Menander ridiculed on the stage the begging priests of Cybele making a living with their noisy cymbals. Apuleius did not spare them. Heraclitus of Ephesus threatened certain partakers of the Eleusinian mysteries with the punishment of fire after death. But it is at least equally clear that the mysteries acted as moral and spiritual forces of no mean efficacy in the Pagan world, and, as the evidence on this point is almost habitually ignored, it is worth some passing attention.

To all about to take part in the mysteries the opening proclamation was: " Every one who has clean

[1] *Fasting*, 16.

hands and a prudent tongue," or "He who is pure from all pollution, and whose soul is conscious of no evil, and who has lived well and justly;" and to such was promised purification from sin.[1] With the mysteries of Mithras were associated baptism by water and fire, penitences, purifications, confessions.[2]

Baptism, indeed, preceded initiation into the mysteries of both Isis and Mithras; it was also in use at the Apollinarian and Eleusinian games; and it was held to be a means of regeneration, and of remission of penalties for sins like perjury.[3] Even infant baptism was an ordinary Roman rite, for Macrobius says that the ninth day after birth, when children were purified (*lustrantur*) and named, was called the *dies lustricus*. At the famous Samothracian mysteries a priest was specially charged with hearing the confessions of great criminals and giving them absolution.[4] The Emperor Julian, in his address to Cybele, refers to the fast which was undergone as a necessary purification of the soul before taking part in the mysteries. Above all, the mysteries held forth the hope or promise of a happy life after death. Plutarch mentions a priest who said that those he initiated were extremely happy after death; and Isocrates speaks of partakers in the mysteries of

[1] Origen, *Against Celsus*, iii. 59.
[2] Denis, *Idées Morales dans l'antiquité*, ii. 281.
[3] Tertullian, *Baptism*, 5.   [4] Boissier, *Religion Romaine*, i. 384.

Ceres as enjoying sweeter hopes thereby about death and eternity.¹ In another work he refers to the just and pious as living with safety in the present and cherishing the sweetest hopes regarding eternity.² Yet with all this evidence, and doubtless much more before him, St. Augustine had the effrontery to declare it to be an idle boast that purity and probity were inculcated by the mysteries,³ and to argue at length and repeatedly against any idea or hope of eternal life as connected with the Pagan religion, still less with the celebration of the mysteries.

It is, moreover, only fair to remember that most of the customs connected with the worst mysteries had symbolical interpretations which redeemed them to some extent from the charge of foolishness or worse that more rational people were apt to bring against them. To take one example: the cymbals used at the mysteries of the Great Mother, or the Earth, the source of all things, bore reference to the noise of iron utensils employed in agriculture; the cymbals were of brass because brass implements were in use before the discovery of iron; and the unbound tamed lion placed at the side of the goddess indicated that no land was too wild or barren to be brought into cultivation. That was Varro's explanation;⁴ and doubtless other absurd or repulsive

¹ Πανηγύρικος, vi.   ² Περὶ εἰρήνης, 12.
³ City of God, ii. 6.   ⁴ Ib. vii. 24.

practices had meanings of this sort which made them acceptable to the mystics of antiquity.

This allegorical or figurative explanation was undoubtedly one of the causes that must account not only for the apparent continuance of the original Pagan theology but for the rapid propagation of foreign creeds. The story of Jupiter and Ceres was let live as an allegory of the Rain and the Earth. The rape of Proserpine by Pluto was taken to allude to the covering of the grain under the clods of the earth; and the Homeric tale of Vulcan detecting Mars and Venus in adultery was made to convey the moral lesson of reason dominating over lust and anger.[1]

So popular did this allegorical tendency become that it was gladly borrowed from the Greeks by the more educated Jews of Alexandria, whose laudable aim it was to reconcile their Mosaic theology with Greek philosophy and with the dictates of human reason. Aristobulus and Philo frankly surrendered the literal truth of Genesis, and rationalised the Scripture stories of Jehovah just as the Greeks had rationalised the Homeric tales of Zeus. Philo is full of such things as that the preference of Jacob to Esau refers to the ultimate prevalence of reason over sense, though later born than sense; that Noah's drunkenness indicates intellectual arrogance; that the daughters of Lot represent the sophisms of the

[1] Arnobius, iv. 33; v. 32, 41.

senses and the imagination. It has not always been noticed how greatly this rationalising spirit, with the liberal scope it afforded to free thought, facilitated the acceptance of Christianity, based as it was on the Hebrew books, especially with that minority of the Pagan philosophers who, like Origen or Clement, became Christian Fathers. Passages in the Scriptures assigning to God hands, feet, or eyes, or attributing to Him resentments and threats, Clement refuses to accept in other than a sacred allegorical sense.[1] The Tree of Life planted in Paradise he takes as allegorical of the Divine prudence.[2] Joseph's coat of many colours of which his brothers stripped him before casting him into the pit signifies lust, which takes its way into the yawning pit.[3] The expulsion of Adam and Eve from Paradise and their clothing themselves with skins contains, according to Origen, the mystical doctrine of the soul losing its wings and being borne down to earth.[4]

The application of this theory to the prophecies led to that extravagant mode of exegesis which has ever since marked this branch of study. It must suffice to quote a very few instances. "The ox and the bear shall come together," said Isaiah (xi. 7). This referred, said Clement, to the conversion of the Jews and Gentiles; the ox or clean animal representing the Jews, and the bear, unclean and wild,

[1] *Stromata*, v. 11.   [2] *Ib.* v. 11.   [3] *Ib.* v. 8.   [4] *Ib.* v. 6.

representing the Gentile. St. Augustine saw in the ram caught by its horns in a thicket, in the story of Abraham and Isaac, a premonition of Christ, who before his sacrifice was crowned with thorns by the Jews.[1] The verse in Habakkuk, "The sun was raised up, and the moon stood still in her course," meant, according to the same writer, that Christ ascended into heaven, and that the Church was established under her King.[2]

It follows from the evidence already given that the central point and best feature of most forms of pre-Christian religion was a strong sense of sin and the desire of an escape from it to a purer life. That an extravagant expression was often given to this sentiment is only what later customs would lead us to expect. The priests who ministered before the idols, clothed in dirty rags, with their hair matted, their nails as long as wild beasts', their bodies totally unwashed,[3] anticipated the theory and almost the practice of the Christian anchorites. The Christian Flagellants had their prototypes in the Pagan fanatics of Plutarch's day, who sat in sackcloth or rags, or rolled about in the mire recounting their sins, or calling out aloud on the vileness of their offences, that rendered them hateful to God and the angels.[4]

---

[1] *City of God*, xvi. 32. [2] *Ib.* xviii. 32.
[3] Clement, *Exhortation to the Heathen*, x.
[4] *On Superstition*, vii.

With regard again to temples, sacrifices, and prayers, the principles of a pious rationalism prevailed widely in the world long before the new faith made its influence felt in the same direction.

Thus Zeno, the founder of the Stoic school, in a lost work called the *Republic*, looked forward to the time when it would no longer be necessary to build temples, and when better things should be regarded as sacred than the mere buildings of human workmen.[1] Seneca considered the whole world to be the only temple worthy of the sublimity of the gods, though admitting that there was so much distinction between sacred and profane, that all things which were lawful under the open sky were not lawful in a temple, and that sacrilege was justly punishable, inasmuch as the offender, albeit he could not by his act injure God, yet did it as if to God.[2] And, in short, Origen's excellent answer to the reproach of Celsus against the Christians for not erecting altars, statues, and temples, that every good man was an altar whose incense was the prayers from a pure conscience, was a reply that completely harmonised with the teaching of rational Paganism.[3]

On no subject has there been more exaggeration than on that of the Pagan idolatry. Celsus ridiculed

---

[1] Plutarch, *Contradictions of Stoics*, vi. ; Clement, *Stromata*, v. 11.   [2] *De Beneficiis*, vii. 7.   [3] viii. 17.

the Christians for saying that images of stone or brass could not be gods, as if any one who was not utterly childish took them for more than offerings consecrated to the gods, or as images serving to represent them.[1] Varro not only declared that the ancient Romans worshipped the gods without an idol for one hundred and seventy years, but complained that the inventors of idols took away the fear of the gods from the people at the same time that they gave a false conception of them.[2] The common argument in defence of the idols was, nor was it without force, that the supposed presence of the gods acted upon many as a deterrent from wickedness; and when Arnobius said that the argument might have been acceptable, had there been in consequence no wicked men upon the earth, the Pagan had the obvious retort that it was precisely to the neglect inculcated by the Christians for the temples and idols of their ancestors that any peculiar wickedness of the time was due.

But for the best statement of the Pagan position with regard to idolatry we must go to Maximus of Tyre, the Platonist. Fully admitting that the gods had no more need of statues or temples than good men had of images, he contended that out of consideration for the utter weakness of man, and because

---

[1] Origen, *Against Celsus*, vii. 62.
[2] Augustine, *City of God*, iv. 31.

the distance between human and divine was as that between earth and heaven, these things had been devised as signs whereby to remember the names of the gods, just as letters had been invented to strengthen human memory, though speech itself had no real need of them. Those whose souls could rise to heaven and unaided grasp the Divine were so few as not to deserve consideration; and on the ground of the human soul being the nearest similitude to God, the Greeks were amply justified in making the images of the gods in human shape. After referring then to the fire-worship of Persia, the animal-worship of Egypt, the oak-worship of Gaul, and the river-worship of Phrygia, he concluded that God, "the Father and Creator of all things, older than Time and Eternity and all-changing Nature, the unnamed Lawgiver," was neither utterable by words nor visible to men's eyes; and that therefore, through their inability to comprehend Him, men had resorted to various names and to the worship of animals, images, plants, hill-tops, or streams, and through their desire to understand Him had attributed to His nature whatever qualities they deemed honourable in their own. And he finished with these words of beautiful toleration : "Only let the Divine be present to the mind, and if the art of Phidias rouse the Greeks to the memory of God, or the worship of animals the Egyptians, or a river some, and fire others, I mind not the discordances, only let them understand, only let them love, only let them remember."[1]

Again, the grand teaching of the Hebrew prophets on the vanity of all but spiritual sacrifice was a familiar topic with the higher minds of Paganism. The most agreeable offering to the gods, said Plutarch, consisted in a right notion of them.[2] It was not, taught Seneca, the sacrifice, but the mind of the sacrificer that signified; it was the pious intentions of the worshipper that honoured the gods, not the richest offerings of victims or gold. Good people might be religious and offer no more than a little corn and pulse, whilst the bad could not escape the consequences of their impiety though they should cover the altars with blood.[3] The gods, he asserted, did good to mankind for the mere pleasure of doing it, unless, forsooth, they could be thought to find an equivalent for their labours in the smoke of entrails and the smell of frankincense.[4] Or what could be finer than this, quoted by Lactantius from a lost work of the same great writer: "Would you think of God as great and gracious and as merciful as He is majestic, as a friend and always at hand, not to be worshipped with sacrifices and outpourings of blood —for what pleasure is there from the slaughter of innocent creatures,—but with a pure soul and a good

[1] *Dissertation* viii.
[2] *Isis and Osiris*, xi.
[3] *De Beneficiis*, i. 6.
[4] *Ib.* iv. 25.

and upright purpose; it is not temples of lofty piles of stones that should be raised to Him, it is in the heart of each man that He should be consecrated."[1] Varro too protested against sacrifices on the ground that the gods neither desired nor asked for them, whilst the false gods made of copper and suchlike, being destitute of feeling, could not care for them.[2] And if we go still farther back, we find the same sort of sentiment. "Think this the best sacrifice and highest worship," wrote Isocrates to Nicocles on the virtues of a king, "to show yourself as good and just as possible." And even Menander, the comedian, could teach on the stage, in days when the stage was the vehicle for the expression of the highest truths, how vain it was to try to propitiate God by sacrifices of bulls and kids, by garments of gold or purple, or by images of ivory or emerald, instead of refraining, from adultery, theft, murder, or covetousness; and declaring that God's delight was in righteous works, could bid his hearers sacrifice to Him by constant justice, and with brightness, not of the dress, but of the heart.[3]

The teaching of Apollonius of Tyana, the Pythagorean, may fitly terminate this part of the subject: "The best and the true way of rendering to the divinity suitable worship, and of conciliating to us

[1] Lactantius, vi. 25.   [2] Arnobius, vii. 1.
[3] Clement, *Stromata*, v. 606.

the favour and goodwill of that God whom we name the First, of that one God separate from the universe, and without whom the other gods remain unknown to us, is not to sacrifice victims to Him, nor to light fire, nor to consecrate to Him any of the things of sense, but always to address to Him the best language, that language which has no need of words, and which is none other than silent thought, pure and unaided intelligence."

Christianity therefore in its opposition to sacrifices, an opposition that must ever count among the most signal of its many services to mankind, simply availed itself of and carried farther a phase of thought that had long been in possession of the world at the time of its appearance. The idea of the abrogation of all further sacrifice after the Crucifixion was of comparatively late growth in the Church; for Gregory the Great spoke of the Eucharist as a " daily sacrifice of immolation"; and Catholicism to this day calls it a sacrifice; but certain allusions by the Fathers to sacrifice seem hardly explicable as mere references to the Lord's Supper. What, for instance, did Clement mean when he wrote : " It is said we ought to go washed to sacrifices and prayers, clean and bright; and that this external adornment and purification are practised for a sign"?[1] Or why should Augustine in the fifth century have protested against persons

---

[1] Clement, *Stromata*, iv. 22.

who maintained that, while visible sacrifices were fitting for other gods, the invisible sacrifice of a pure mind and a holy will was suitable to God; and have argued that visible sacrifices were signs of the invisible, and that, as in prayer and praise words were offered to God, so in sacrifice there was a visible offering to Him to whom in our hearts we should present ourselves as an invisible sacrifice?[1] or why, again, in defending his co-religionists against the charge of worshipping martyrs, should he have said : " Who ever heard a priest of the faithful, at an altar built for the honour and worship of God over the holy body of some martyr, say in prayer, 'I offer to thee a sacrifice, O Peter, Paul, or Cyprian,' since it is to God that sacrifices are offered at their tombs "?[2] The sacrifices alluded to in these and similar passages refer, it is said, to the Eucharist; but even if so, the Christian character thus given to the sacrifice did not prevent it from being surrounded with the same ideas which attached to that form of religious ceremony in the Pagan worship; and the sacrifices offered at the tombs of the martyrs appear to have borne a much closer resemblance to those offered by the Pagans at the tombs of their dead at the Parentalia than is implied by the language of St. Augustine.

But the difficulty is extreme of trying to institute

[1] *City of God*, x. 19.
[2] *Ib.* viii. 27. Compare Cyprian, *Ep.* 33, 36.

any comparison between Christianity and Paganism in the matter of superstition. We may, however, lessen it by drawing a distinction between the higher and the lower Paganism. Instead of comparing the higher Christianity with the lower Paganism —a course which has vitiated so many conclusions— we shall be more likely to hit the truth by contrasting only the different levels with one another, in other words, only the higher with the higher and the lower with the lower. The higher Christianity and the higher Paganism may be at once cancelled as equally exempt from and superior to superstition; so that the comparison in this regard remains to be determined between the lower Christianity and the lower Paganism. Was the former an improvement on the latter in the matter of superstitious observances?

Can we answer this in the affirmative when we recall the history of Catholicism? or when we think even of its present condition in many parts of the world? One can only hint at the answer, without venturing on a dogmatic decision; but at least the doubt is justifiable whether the difference in this respect was so very great between any country in its Catholic and in its previous Pagan state; whether, in short, as a result of the change, superstition came very much to diminish in quantity or even to differ in degree, till at least the period of the Reformation in the countries affected thereby.

CHAPTER V

THE PAGAN BELIEF IN HEAVEN

"ALL will admit that we have a soul," says Seneca, "but what that soul is which rules and governs us no one will explain to you any more than where it is situate; one will call it a spirit, another a certain harmony, another a divine force and part of God, another very thin air, another incorporeal power, nor will there be wanting others to call it even blood or heat."[1]

At most he is content to call it himself a certain kind of spirit (*quodam modo se habens spiritus*).[2]

And to the present day we can define it no better. All we know of it is still its existence, not its nature.

The most generally received belief in antiquity about the soul of man was that it was an emanation from the Divine Soul, something of heavenly origin, and thereby constituting the link by virtue of which all men might acknowledge God as their Father, and

[1] *Naturales Quaestiones*, vii. 25.   [2] *Epist.* 50.

speak of themselves as the sons of God. "The ancients thought," says Macrobius, "that souls were given by Jupiter, and returned to him again after death."

This belief in the divine nature of the soul, and in the fatherly relation of God to man, supplied a constant and forcible motive for virtuous living and purity of thought to an extent that has been seldom appreciated. Seneca, with his purely Pagan training, says, "Unless the soul is pure and holy it cannot receive God."[1] "If a man," says Epictetus, "could worthily realise this opinion, that we are all in a special sense the children of God, and that God is the Father both of men and gods, I imagine he would think nothing mean or vulgar about himself"; and he goes on to regret that so many men, thinking more of that lower relationship which, by virtue of the body, connected them with the animals, than of that which, by virtue of the soul, connected them with God, esteemed themselves wretched instead of highly favoured. He would have every man remember, in eating, or in conversation, or in anything else, not only that he in a sense carries God within him, but that as the special work of God it behoves him not to dishonour his Maker: "Being the work of such an artificer, do you dishonour Him? And not only did He make you, but He gave you in charge and

[1] *Epist.* 87.   [2] *Discourses*, i. 3.

trust to yourself alone. Will you not even remember this, but also dishonour your trust? But if God gave an orphan into your charge, you would not so neglect him; yet He has given yourself to yourself, and says, I had no one more trustworthy than yourself, keep him for me such as he was born, reverent, faithful, high-minded, unperturbed, free from passions and disturbance."[1] From the same doctrine flowed the other Stoic doctrine, subsequently borrowed by Christians, of the brotherhood of all men, and the consequent duty of a charitable bearing towards all men, even towards slaves: "Slave yourself, will you not bear with your own brother, who has Zeus for his progenitor, and is like a son from the same beginnings and of the same descent from above? . . . Will you not remember who you are and whom you rule? that they are kinsmen, that they are brethren by nature, that they are the offspring of Zeus."[2]

Christianity never inculcated a higher teaching, nor ever supplied higher motives to virtue than we thus see to have been inculcated and supplied by the schools of Pagan philosophy. Nor must we restrict the influence of those schools to the narrow limits sometimes suggested by the complaints of the Pagans themselves. If Seneca complained of the general desertion or neglect of philosophy, it was probably as preachers have in all ages complained of the

[1] *Discourses*, ii. 8. [2] *Ib.* i. 13.

numbers or zeal of their audience. At all events we have the admission of Origen that the philosophers did not pick their hearers, but conversed in public with all or any who cared to listen to them; that they invited the young to their lectures, and encouraged them, often with much success, to exchange a bad life for a better; and that they sought to make even slaves learners of philosophy.[1] Surely their influence cannot have been contemptible, if it produced teachers like Epictetus, or propagated teaching like that of Epictetus over every city and country of the civilised world. Nor is there any doubt but that this is what it did do.

The doctrine that the soul was an emanation from the Divine mind, and that its ultimate lot was to be reabsorbed in the same on its emancipation from the body, and that in this sense the soul was immortal, was a belief which, descended originally from the Brahminical theosophy of India, was widely spread over the world at the appearance of Christianity. It constituted the faith and hope of the whole educated Pagan world; and in consequence of it, Plato and Seneca and Maximus of Tyre learnt to speak of the body in its relation to the soul in precisely the same language that was common to the Buddhists or the Gnostics. "Our soul," says Seneca, "will then have cause to rejoice when, sent forth from these shades in

[1] *Against Celsus*, iii. 51, 54.

which it is immersed, it shall see things no longer dimly, but with the light of perfect day, and shall have been restored to its heaven, and shall have received the place which is its birthplace."[1] Or again, "The body is the prison and chain of the soul, and is tossed hither and thither, the sport of punishments and robberies and diseases, but the soul is sacred and eternal, nor can any man lay his hands upon it."[2] So general was this belief that we even find Titus assuring his soldiers at the siege of Jerusalem that the souls of those that fell in battle would be received by the pure ether and have their place among the stars.

Maximus of Tyre is a good exponent of the same belief: "The generous soul is not averse to the destruction of the body, but looks forward to its liberty and to the pure light of heaven with as much delight as the prisoner sees fall the walls of his prison. Flesh and bones are to the soul but the apparel of a day, which the soul, if good, neglects, and from which it only desires to be released as quickly as possible."[3] "What men call death therefore is the beginning of immortality, when the soul is called up to its own place, to enter on a new life."[4] "And when the soul has thus departed from earth to heaven (ἐνθένδε ἐκεῖσε), and has cast off the body and left it to corrupt in the earth, from constituting a man,

[1] *Epist.* 79.   [2] *Ib.* 16.   [3] *Discourses*, 13.   [4] *Ib.* 14.

it becomes a demon (or angel), and beholds with pure eyes sights appropriate to it, being no longer obscured by the flesh nor disturbed by the senses. In that condition it looks back with pity on its former life, and rejoices in its present existence, commiserating those other souls whom it has left on earth, and desiring from its love towards them to attend upon and support them." [1]

Nothing therefore is falser than the common notion that in pre-Christian times men died without hope. Otherwise how could Maximus have written as follows : " How can a man swim out and behold God ? In brief, thou shalt then behold Him when thou art called to Him, and thou shalt be called in no long time; await the summons. Old age shall come to lead thee, and death, of which the coward bewails and dreads the approach, but which the lover of God receives gladly and courageously."

According to the same author, Pythagoras was the first among the Greeks to say that, though man's body would die, his soul would fly upwards, to dwell, immortal and insensible of time, where it existed originally. According to Cicero, however, the first teacher of the soul's immortality was Pherecydes, the Syrian, of whom Pythagoras was the disciple.[2] But this is merely an antiquarian point. The important thing is the antiquity of the belief, connected with

[1] *Discourses*, 15.   [2] *Tusc.* i. 16.

which Macrobius mentions a remarkable ancient custom, whereby a holy man might rightfully be killed, that his soul might the sooner return to the gods. "Those souls," he says, "which for their sanctity it was thought could be sent to Heaven, they were willing should be released from the body and go thither as soon as possible."[1] At all events from the time of Pythagoras the belief in the survival of the soul was as prevalent in the world as the alternative theory of the essential unity of the soul and body, and of the extinction of one with the other.

It must suffice to give typical illustrations of this belief, as a substitute for a complete collection of the evidence. Cicero may without doubt be taken as fairly expressing the common faith of his time in the dream of Scipio that occurs in the sixth book of his *Republic*, wherein Paulus Scipio instructs his son Publius how in Heaven there is a certain definite place where all who have served their country, or cultivated music or other divine studies with great ability, enjoy a blessed existence. "Of a truth they enjoy real life who have flown from the chains of their bodies as from a prison; but that which you call life is death." The road to Heaven is by the cultivation of justice, and by piety towards one's relations and neighbours and country; but the souls

[1] iii. 7 : animas quas sacras in coelum mitti posse arbitrati sunt, viduatas corpore quam primum illo ire voluerunt.

of those who are given up to pleasure and who violate the laws of gods and men hover round the earth on quitting the body, nor return to Heaven till after the lapse of ages. In another treatise Cicero says: "If aught should make it appear to be indicated by God that we should depart from life, let us obey joyfully and thankfully, and let us think that we are dismissed from prison and released from our chains, either to return to that eternal home which is clearly meant for us, or to be free from henceforth from all sensation and trouble."[1] So he speaks of our hope of a happier life than the present,[2] and, calling our life here death, says we shall only then really live when we have come to that heavenly life hereafter.[3]

In the sense of man being thus by nature an inheritor of Heaven, a writer as old as Empedocles speaks of him as a pilgrim, a stranger, and an exile; insinuating, says Plutarch, by the soft name of pilgrimage the origin of the soul, that it came to us from above.[4] "Endowed with pious mind," says Epicharmus, the comic poet, "you will not in dying suffer aught evil; the spirit will dwell in Heaven above."[5] This was the general, if not the universal, Pagan belief. Cicero alludes to Socrates conversing, just before he drank the poison, as if he were about, not to be put to a compulsory death, but to ascend

---

[1] *Tusc.* i. 49.   [2] *Ib.* i. 34.   [3] *Ib.* i. 31.
[4] *On Banishment*, xvii.   [5] Clement, *Stromata*, iv. 26.

to Heaven.[1] If the belief was not expressed upon the Pagan tombs, we know from every consolation addressed to bereaved friends that it was firmly impressed upon their hearts. It is the hope expressed in the consolation by Seneca to Marcia for the death of her son, or to Polybius on the death of his brother, or by Plutarch to Apollonius on the loss of his son. He has only, says Plutarch, made a digression from this life to eternity, and if, as is probable, it is true that honours and dignity await the righteous after death, Apollonius should cherish very high hopes for his son. Elsewhere Plutarch refers to the joy lost by the Epicureans in not looking forward to a reunion with their dear departed ones. If the dead feel not, Seneca argues with Polybius, his brother has been restored to the place where he was before birth, and has no more to fear or desire or suffer; but if the soul survives the body, his brother, freed as it were from a long imprisonment, rejoices to contemplate the great spectacle of Nature, and to look down on human affairs from a higher standpoint, but with a much clearer insight into heavenly things; at length he is free, safe, and eternal, enjoying the free and open Heaven, raised up to that place, wherever it is, which receives souls that have cast their chains, and where he wanders at will, beholding with the greatest rapture all the wonders of Nature. It were an error

[1] *Tusc.* i. 30.

to think he has lost the light; on the contrary, he has gained a more certain light; and on the journey we have all to undertake, he has only gone before, not forsaken us.

He assures Marcia that only the image of her son has perished, but that he himself is eternal and in the enjoyment of a better condition, since the soul and the flesh are in constant warfare on earth, the soul perpetually striving to regain its birthplace, where eternal peace awaits it. Her son, after a short sojourn above the earth, there to be purged of the inherent vices of the mortal state, has been raised to the heights of Heaven, where he wanders in company with the Scipios and Catos and other souls of the blessed, and learns with certainty to understand the ways of the stars and all the most intimate secrets of Nature. Sometimes, with Marcia's own father, he looks down on earth; for which reason their survivor should not only blush to do any mean or ignoble action, but also refrain from weeping for those who have undergone a change for the better.

When therefore we are told that before Christianity men died without hope of any future life, we are confronted with this fact that the fragmentary literature of Pagan times bears striking evidence of that hope on almost every page. That the body acted as a restraint on the soul; that death was the soul's escape to a purer life of contemplation and knowledge; that the scene of that purer life was in Heaven; and that parted friends would there be reunited,—these were the cardinal points of Pagan belief, which Christianity did no more than inherit. We have the statement of Apuleius that to all who died after a just life the expression *Manes deus* was applied for the sake of honour,[1] and this was apparently all that was really meant by the apotheosis of the Roman emperors. The senate decreed them divine honours, that is, gave expression to the hope or belief that they had gone to Heaven, much as in later times the Christian Church canonised its saints, whom she as often called Divi as Sancti. It was therefore with no shock to Christian feeling that Constantine and his successors were divinised by the senate, and had temples raised and priests appointed to them; and if with the Emperor Gratian the custom ceased, the Christian emperors were for some time afterwards still spoken of as gods.[2] It was in this way that Cicero believed all the gods of antiquity to have arisen, and his question accorded with the popular belief: "Is not almost the whole of Heaven filled with the human race?"[3] And, speaking generally of the dead, Seneca says to Marcia, "We have sent them away, nay rather, have sent them on before us, and we shall follow them." Often his expressions

---

[1] *Golden Ass*, xi.   [2] Boissier, *Religion Romaine*, i. 5.
[3] *Tusc.* i. 13.

might be taken for a Christian's, as where he speaks of our life here as the prelude to a better and longer life, as a preparation for another birth; or where he says, "Another origin awaits us and another condition of things"; or exclaims, "That day which you dread as your last is the birthday of eternity."[1]

According to Cicero, the Stoics only believed in a future life that would be long, but not immortal. But the Stoics never formulated any uniform system of belief, and as far as we can judge from their language, some believed in immortality, and some in no future life at all. The belief in immortality was nevertheless common to most sects of philosophy, and to the general mass of the people in the later days of Paganism.

The strength and vividness of the belief are proved by the story of Cleombrotus, who, after reading the *Phaedo* of Plato, was seized with so great a desire for the immortality therein foreshadowed, that, bidding the sun farewell, he leapt from a high wall to certain destruction.[2] A somewhat similar effect was produced by the teaching of the neo-Platonist Plotinus upon his pupil Porphyry; the latter being so possessed with the idea of a disembodied existence that, but for the dissuasion of his master, he would have starved himself out of the world.

[1] *Epist.* 102.
[2] Callimachus, *Epig.* 24. Cicero, *Tusc. Quaest.* v. 34, 84.

The arguments on which the Pagans based their belief in the soul's immortality are of less importance than the fact that subsequent reasoning has added no single fresh one to those they adduced. By vast numbers of men, not of course by all, the doctrine that after death men's purified souls enjoyed endless felicity was accepted without doubt; and of such force were the well-known arguments in its favour, that even a Christian writer like Lactantius, seeking to demonstrate the immortality of the soul, based it entirely on the old Platonic arguments about the nature of the soul and of virtue, without once referring to the resurrection of Christ.[1]

Another Christian writer, Arnobius, bears striking testimony to the universality of the belief, and reveals the Church in an attitude of opposition towards it. As a Christian, he protests against the common notions of the divine origin and consequently immortal nature of the soul. "What man," he asks, "who, when he hears it said by the wisest that the soul is immortal, would not throw himself headlong into all manner of vices and fearlessly set about unlawful things? How shall he be overcome by any fear who has been persuaded that he is immortal?"[2] He says to the Pagans: "You rest the salvation of

[1] *Divine Institutes*, vii. 18.
[2] ii. 29. Tatian in his address to the Greeks (c. 13) makes a similar protest against the natural immortality of the soul.

your souls upon yourselves, and are assured that by your own exertions alone you become gods. . . . You think that as soon as you pass away, freed from the bonds of your carnal members, you will find wings wherewith you may rise to Heaven and to the stars."[1]

Here we have as clearly expressed as it could be the difference between the teaching of Philosophy and of Christianity on the future destiny of the soul; and an admission that the view which came to be deemed orthodox was a limitation of that theretofore entertained in the world. But it is evident from the second quotation from Arnobius that the immortality promised by Philosophy was not dissociated from moral virtue and exertion. It has already been shown from Cicero, that only after the lapse of ages were the bad thought capable of admission to Heaven. Even so, Catholicism offered nothing better. And Plutarch speaks of those who have led pious and just lives as especially entitled to look forward to rewards after death, and of such hopes as constituting strong incentives to virtue.[2] Clement himself admits that the barbarian wisdom was well acquainted with the hope after death,—a good hope to the good, but to the bad the reverse.[3] So that when Dean Milman, seeking to correct Gibbon, speaks of notions

[1] ii. 33.   [2] *Pleasure according to Epicurus*, 26.
[3] *Stromata*, iv. 22.

of future retribution and of the life after death as operating on the thoughts and feelings, and sometimes on the actions of Christians, in a way that constituted a profound difference between Christian and Pagan polytheism, it is certain that he must have forgotten or ignored the abundance of classical testimony which reduces that difference to a minimum.

The only real difference between Christian and Pagan thought regarded the future fate of the body, not that of the soul. Regarding as he did the body as impure, as partaking of the evil that lay in every form of matter, the Pagan looked generally to a future existence which should be purely spiritual, to a life emancipated from, and no longer trammelled by, the body. For this reason anti-Christian writers like Celsus and Porphyry protested against and opposed the Christian dogma of the resurrection of the body,—a dogma, which from the point of view of the essential antagonism between soul and body, spirit and matter, appeared to them to bind together for all eternity the pure with the impure. But the idea of a corporeal resurrection was itself no new one in the world; for the prediction of the ultimate resurrection of the dead, at the coming of Soshyos, the Saviour, was not only one of the peculiar tenets of the Persian Zoroastrian religion, but it even found some favour in the Greek schools of philosophy. Pliny, who disbelieved in a future life of any sort, speaks with some contempt of the hope of Democritus in a future state for the body;[1] and, if Clement may be credited, Heraclitus and those of the Stoics who shared his belief in a final purification of the world by fire, held that each individual would rise again exactly as he was before.[2]

It is also noticeable that many of the early Christians themselves accepted or explained the resurrection of the body in an allegorical sense, making it to refer, for instance, to the flight or escape of the soul from the bondage of the body, which was, as it were, its prison or grave; or again, to the restoration through baptism from the death of ignorance to real truth.[3] And it was characteristic of most of the Gnostic Christians to deny the resurrection of the body, and only to believe in the future life of the soul, Tertullian asserting such denial and belief of such heretics as Marcion, Basilides, Carpocrates, Valentinus, Marcus, Cerdo, and Apelles.[4] Provided the soul were immortal, they regarded as indifferent the fate of the body.

There is yet another point on which the Pagan could have seen no reason to prefer the Christian teaching. He habitually poured libations and made

[1] *Nat. Hist.* vii. 56 : reviviscendi promissa Democrito vanitas.
[2] *Stromata*, v. 1. Compare Athenagoras, *Apol.* 36.
[3] Tertullian, *Resurrection of the Flesh*, 19.
[4] *Ib. Against Heresies.*

sacrifices for the dead in order to benefit their future lot. But for dead children no libations nor sacrifices were offered, for the reason that it was thought an impious thing to lament those whose souls passed immediately to a better and diviner state. The Christian, on the other hand, to his everlasting shame, held and taught that innocent infants, if they died unbaptized, passed at once and for ever to a state of misery, of which no human mind could form any conception, amid dungeons and tortures and flames. "Hold most firmly, and by no means doubt," wrote St. Fulgentius, "that little children, whether they die before or after birth, pass, without the holy sacrament of baptism, from this world, to be punished with the everlasting punishment of eternal fire." This was for ages, and, for the majority of the Christian world, is still the orthodox doctrine; a fact which goes far to explain how it came to pass that to the more intellectual classes of antiquity the teaching of the Church never commended itself, and that Philosophy never yielded its allegiance to, and still raises its protest against, its creed, which, making such a doctrine its fundamental basis and starting-point, replunged the world into grosser and more terrific superstitions than any it displaced, and reduced human reason to so miserable a level, that its total and universal extinction seemed at one time as desirable as it seemed imminent.

CHAPTER VI

THE PAGAN BELIEF IN HELL

HAVING shown in the last chapter that with regard to the belief in Heaven, in the immortality of the soul, in the reunion of the dead, and in a future retribution, the Pagan world differed from the Christian in nothing save in the grounds for such beliefs, it remains to show that with regard also to the darker side of the faith in a future life, Christianity imported into the world no essentially novel doctrine. The Indian ideas of Hell, surpassing in horror anything with which the imagination of Christian monks and Fathers familiarised Europe, had been current in the world long before the oldest Greek literature; and to the infernal torments of the popular Greek and Latin faith, of which we get clear enough indications in Homer and Plato and Virgil, an Indian or Egyptian origin may with much probability be assigned. At all events, the ideas of a judgment and punishment after death were common to India, Assyria, Egypt, Persia, Greece, and Italy, for very many centuries before Christianity, so that Celsus used a perfectly fair argument against the new faith when he objected to the Christian doctrines of a resurrection, of a judgment, of rewards for the just, and of fire for the unjust, that they were stale (ἕωλα) opinions.[1] He says to the Christians: "Just as you believe in eternal punishments, so do the priests, who interpret and initiate into the sacred mysteries."[2] And again, when he is protesting against the idea of a corporeal resurrection: "I shall address those who hope for the enjoyment of eternal life with God through their soul or mind ... and they are rightly persuaded that those who live well shall be blessed, and the unrighteous shall all suffer everlasting punishment."[3]

Clearly, therefore, the belief not merely in future punishment, but in everlasting punishment, belonged to the Pagan creed before it passed over into the Christian religion. Plutarch on this point confirms the evidence of Celsus when he refers to persons who regarded death as an evil on account of *eternal* torments and horrible punishments suffered underground in Hell.[4] And in another place he argues against the Epicureans, that men will not be at all happier than brutes for mere unconcern at the stories

[1] Origen, *Against Celsus*, ii. 5.   [2] *Ib.* viii. 48.
[3] *Ib.* viii. 49: αἰωνίοις κακοῖς.
[4] *On Moral Virtue*, x.: τιμωρίαις αἰωνίοις ὑπὸ γῆν. The Greek word in Celsus and Plutarch is the same as in the New Testament for *everlasting*.

of Hell, and for not fearing endless sorrows and *everlasting* torments hereafter.¹ The hope, he contends, entertained by the common people of an eternal existence exceeds in pleasure their dread of Hell; and when they lose their wives, children, or friends, they would prefer to think of them as existing even in misery than as for ever annihilated.²

The popular belief was sustained in antiquity, as it has been since, by the skill of the artist and by the influence of the stage. "Often have I seen pictures of the manifold torments of Acheron," Plautus makes an actor say in one of his plays.³ And Pausanias describes a picture by Polygnotus, wherein some of the punishments of the underworld were vividly displayed.⁴ On the stage we catch glimpses of the same thing, as in the following fragment ascribed to Philemon or to Diphilus, both comedians, wherein it is urged that the dead do not escape the Deity:—

> "There is an eye of Justice, which sees all.
> For two ways we think to Hades lead,
> One for the just, the other for the impious.
> But if the earth hides both for ever,
> Go rob, steal, plunder, riot.
> But be not deceived, for there is a judgment in Hades,
> Which God, the Lord of all, will execute;
> Whose name I dare not mention,

---

¹ *Of Pleasure according to Epicurus*, 8.   ² *Ib.* 26.
³ *Captivorum*, v. 4. 1.   ⁴ x. 28.

Who gives to sinners length of life.
If any mortal thinks that day by day
While doing ill he eludes the gods' keen sight
His thoughts are evil, and when Justice has
The leisure, he shall then be detected
So thinking. Look, whoe'er you be that say
That there is not a God. There is, there is.
If one by nature evil does evil
Let him redeem the time, for such as he
Shall by-and-by due punishment receive."

The dream of Thespesius, in the treatise by Plutarch, *On the Slowness of God to Punish*, reveals a popular conception of future punishment in Hell that fully equals the most horrible imaginings of the Buddhist or the Christian. The demons, plunging the souls of the avaricious into a lake of molten gold, and then, when almost consumed by the furnace, transferring them to an equally cold lake of lead, thence to a lake of iron, and thence back again to the lake of molten gold, prove that the Pagans had nothing further to learn on this head, and, moreover, that they anticipated the Christians in the evil connotation which ultimately came to be the sole one with reference to the word demon. It is unnecessary to do more than refer to the well-known story of Er, with which Plato ends his *Republic*, and seeks to connect the pursuit of virtue or vice on earth with either glorious rewards in Heaven after death or with the most dreadful torments in Hell.

Even Zeno, the founder of the Stoic school, taught that the good and bad were separated in the underworld; the former in pleasant regions, the latter in dark and miry places.[1] Lucian in his *True History*, or imaginary visit to the other world, wherein he refers to the five islands, with fires ever burning on them, as the habitations of the wicked, or to three rivers of mire, blood, and fluid fire respectively, meant to ridicule not the Christian, but the common Pagan belief, as is proved by another passage where he protests against the poets for the tortures, *fires*, and devouring vultures with which they threatened the unfortunate dead.

Death itself, says Plutarch, puts no end to the fears of the superstitious man, for superstition extends his fears beyond the grave, and adds the imagination of immortal, never-ending, evil after the sorrows of this life. "I know not what gates of Hell open themselves from beneath, rivers of fire and Stygian torments; a gloomy darkness appears, full of ghastly spectres and horrid shapes, with dreadful sights and doleful groans, and judges and tormentors, full of millions of miseries and woes."[2] The Christians had no better explanation to offer for the resemblance between the heathen notions and their own than the utterly unsound one of plagiarism. "We get ourselves laughed at," says Tertullian, "for proclaiming that God will one day judge the world. For, like

[1] Lactantius, vii. 7. [2] *Superstition*, 4.

THE PAGAN BELIEF IN HELL 113

us, the poets and philosophers set up a judgment-seat in the realms below. And if we threaten Gehenna, which is a reservoir of secret fire under the earth for the purposes of punishment, we are laughed to scorn (*decachinnamur*). For so too they have their Pyriphlegethon, a river of flame in the regions of the dead. And if we speak of Paradise . . . the Elysian plains have taken possession of their faith. Whence is it that you have all this so like us in the poets and philosophers? The reason simply is that they have been taken from our religion."[1] We may admit the similarity, but we shall be nearer the truth if we reverse the explanation and make the Christian belief derivative from the Pagan, not the Pagan from the Christian. But a passage from the Christian Arnobius will establish beyond all possibility of cavil the argument that in their doctrine of Hell and everlasting future punishment the Christians rather intensified the popular belief of ages than taught any new thing regarding it. "Do you dare laugh at us," he asks, "when we speak of Hell and unquenchable fires? . . . Does not your Plato speak of Acheron, Styx, Cocytus, and Pyriphlegethon, and assert that in them souls are rolled along, engulfed, and burned up? . . . This is man's real death when souls which know not God shall be consumed in long-protracted torments with raging

[1] *Apologeticus*, 47.

fire, into which certain fiercely cruel beings shall cast them, unknown before Christ and brought to light only by His wisdom."[1]

Clearly therefore the early Christians, at least as interpreted by Arnobius, regarded their faith in Hell as something far more fearful than had theretofore haunted human imagination. We know from Celsus and Plutarch that their claim to originality with regard to the *everlasting* duration of future punishment cannot be allowed; but at least they had the will and the intention to preach a doctrine on this subject which should appeal more cogently to the superstitious fears of mankind; and it would even appear that this very fact was one of the causes of their rapid success. Origen, for example, speaks of converts to Christianity despising every kind of torture and even death through their fears of what was called in the Word everlasting punishments; nor was it the very wicked so much as people of average morality who were so affected.[2] One of the charges brought by Celsus against the Christians was their resort to this religious terrorism, though he deprecated the idea of himself rejecting the doctrine of the future punishment of the wicked, and of the reward of the good.[3] Celsus was perfectly justified in this charge, for the teaching of the new creed undid all that Philosophy had achieved in the way of emancipating men's

[1] ii. 4.   [2] *Against Celsus*, iii. 78.   [3] *Ib.* iii. 16.

minds from the degrading fears of cruel and purposeless tortures after death.

Although Plutarch appears to defend the belief in Hell against the Epicureans, he admits that not many believed in the stories about it, and himself speaks of them as the tenets of old women, or as the fables of mothers and nurses. "Almost every one knows," he says, "that the stories about the dead are suited to popular apprehensions, and that spectres and phantasms of burning rivers and horrible regions and tortures with frightful names are all mixed with fable and fiction as poison with food."[1]

This result was distinctly the work of philosophy, for which even antagonistic schools, like the Stoics and Epicureans, worked together. "No one," says Seneca, "is such a child as to be afraid of Cerberus and the shades."[2] He reminds Marcia that the dead are afflicted by no evil, that the representations of the lower regions as terrible are the fables of poets, and subterranean shades and prisons and rivers of fire and dread tribunals only fictions invented for the terror of mankind. In the same way Cicero calls them the horrors (*portenta*) of the poets and painters.[3] There was no difference in this respect between Seneca and Lucretius, between Epictetus and Epicurus. "When God," says Epictetus, "gives a man the signal for retreat from life, and bids a man come, whither is it that

[1] *De audiendis Poetis*, ii. [2] *Epist.* 24. [3] *Tusc. Quaest.* i. 5, 6, 21.

he is called? To nothing terrible, but to the place whence he came, to his friends and kinsmen, and to the elements, whatever was in him of fire or earth or air or water returning to its respective element, but to no Hades, nor Acheron, nor Pyriphlegethon."[1]

Philosophy either denied in this way the existence of Hell altogether, or explained it away as a figurative expression for the human body or the condition of the soul, much as the Broad Church school of our times is wont to do. "It was this body," says Macrobius of the philosophers, "that they called the sepulchre of the soul, the cave of Dis, or Hell; and all that a fabulous mode of thinking held to happen there, they tried to assign to ourselves, and to our human bodies; asserting that the River of Oblivion was nothing else than the straying of a soul, which forgot the majesty of its former existence that it had before it was compelled to live in a body, and which thought its corporeal life to be its only one. By a similar interpretation they taught that Phlegethon signified the heats of anger and desires; that Acheron signified whatever we repented having done or said; that Styx was whatever drowned men's souls in the whirlpool of mutual hatred; and that the vulture devouring an imperishable liver alluded to the torments of conscience."[2]

From the point of view therefore inculcated by

[1] iii. 13. [2] i. 10.

Philosophy, death presented only two possible alternatives, one of them bright with hope, and the other at least exempt from terror. For it meant either the transference of the soul to a better life, or the close of all human ills in what Seneca calls a great and eternal peace. Seneca's ideas on the happier alternative have already been quoted; his ideas on the other were such as afford an obvious consolation to human reason still. He argues that if death replaces us in the tranquil state we enjoyed before birth, it were as reasonable to pity the `not-yet-born as the already dead. To die in that case was simply not to be, wherein, if there were any torment, we must have felt it also before we were born. What more foolish than to think it were worse for a lamp after it was put out than before it was lit; and were not we too, like lamps, lighted and extinguished, suffering indeed somewhat between while, but enjoying profound security at either term?[1]

In the same spirit Cicero makes Cato say of death, that either it is to be regarded as a matter of no concern, if it entirely extinguishes the soul, or to be wished for, if it conducts the soul to a place where it is to exist for all eternity. "Any third possibility can certainly not be found."[2] Marcus Aurelius says to himself: "Thou hast embarked and made the voyage and come to shore, so get out; if indeed to another

[1] *Epist.* 54. [2] *De Senectute,* xix.

life, there is no want of gods even there, but if to a state of unconsciousness, thou wilt cease to be held in bondage by pleasure and pains."[1] "Who fears death either fears the loss of sensation or a different kind of sensation; but if thou shalt have no sensation, neither wilt thou feel any harm, and if thou shalt have another kind of sensation, thou wilt be a different kind of being and wilt not cease to live."[2] Though he would look on death as, at its worst, a natural process, a dissolution of the body into its elements, and therefore nothing to be afraid of, his moral sense clearly rebelled against the darker alternative. Was it possible that the gods who had arranged all things well and benevolently for mankind should suffer it that the best men, who had held most communion with divinity, should after their death never exist again, but be completely extinguished? His reply is the humble but faithful one of sound human reason, that if it were so, the gods would have ordered it otherwise had it been for the best, and that their ordering of it either way should be implicitly trusted.[3] There is no indication that Epictetus believed in any conscious survival of the soul after its separation from the body. Like Aurelius, he compares life to a voyage, and proceeds thus: "What can I do? Choose the captain, the sailors, the day, the time. Then a storm comes on.

[1] ii. 3.   [2] viii. 58.   [3] xii. 5.

What more care then have I, who have done my part? The business is now another's—the captain's. But the ship is sinking. What then have I to do? I only do what I can, I drown without fear, not screaming, nor accusing God, but with the knowledge that what has been produced must also perish, for I am not eternal (αἰών) but a man, a part of the whole as an hour is part of the day. I must be present like the hour and pass like the hour."[1]

Yet in face of such a conclusion, leading logically on high authority to a mere life of sensual pleasure, no one ever upheld more firmly than Epictetus the beacon of virtuous and noble conduct as an end in itself worth living for, even though death should be its absolute termination, nor any remembrance nor reward be in store for it. "Why should not a man," asks Aurelius, "wait tranquilly for his end, whether it be extinction or removal elsewhere, content till then to reverence and bless the gods, to do good to men, and to practise toleration and self-restraint?"[2] He would have himself end his journey with content, like a ripe olive that falls to the ground, blessing Nature which produced it, and thanking the tree on which it grew.[3]

How different all this from the teaching of the Christian Lactantius, who argues that the pursuit of virtue without the hope of immortality is the greatest folly, and that, but for the compensation of everlast-

[1] *Discourses*, ii. 5.   [2] v. 33.   [3] iv. 48.

ing life, virtue with all its hardships cannot be deemed a good thing at all![1]

One would fain dwell longer on the philosophical treatment of this great problem, so awful is the contrast between it and the teaching of the fanatics, who, claiming to represent the religion of Christ, which they were less capable of understanding than of misinterpreting, revived, with superadded terrors, the old Pagan notions of Hell, and plunged the world back into mental barbarism. It is almost enough to make one despair of human sanity to think that some seven centuries after Epicurus such a book should have been written as the twenty-first of Augustine's *City of God.* Conceive one of the greatest luminaries of the Catholic Church arguing from the nature of the salamander, and from the supposed antiseptic nature of the peacock, in favour of the possibility of human bodies lasting for ever in burning flames; contending that a God who could perform such a miracle as to create the world with all its countless miracles of earth and sky, could easily cause the bodies of the dead not only to rise but to be susceptible of torment in everlasting fire; maintaining that the same material fire of Hell will be equally adapted to prey upon the solid bodies of men and the aerial bodies of devils; and suggesting that in that eternal fire the due proportion may be

[1] vi. 8.

observed between punishment and desert by the graduation of the temperature of the fire to individual cases, or by different degrees of sensibility to the intensity of the torment!

It is surely time that a man who could descend to such appalling nonsense as this should come down from the pedestal he has occupied for so long as the most philosophical of the Christian Fathers! It is a profanation to philosophy to mention it in connection with him. But the speculation was a favourite one with most of the early Christian writers, and must affect our estimate of their intellectual calibre. Lactantius, who deserted philosophy for the Church, describes the wicked rising with indestructible bodies, capable of holding out against tortures and everlasting fire, a fire so far unlike the earthly element that it is self-fed, and fluid like water, and in no danger of being extinguished for want of sustenance![1] Minucius Felix, speaking of the endlessness of Hell-torments, says, "The intelligent fire burns limbs and restores them, feeds on them, and nourishes them."[2] Cyprian regards it as sure to be the great compensating joy for believers at the Day of Judgment that "an ever-burning Gehenna will burn up the condemned, and a punishment devouring with living flames; nor will there be any source whence at any time they may have either respite or end to their torments.

[1] vi. 21. [2] *Octavius*, 35.

Souls with their bodies will be reserved in infinite tortures."[1]

There is no need to quote more of the repulsive evidence, which proves that real and material fire was, as it still is among most of the sects, an essential belief of historical Christianity, and that all figurative relaxations, either as to the nature or duration of that fire-penalty, such as from time to time have been ventured on by Christians like Origen or John Erigena, are genuine heretical departures from the original Christian faith. Strange to say, the vividness of the revised or intensified belief appears to have been one of the contributory causes to the rapid propagation of the faith, partly from the sheer influence of terror, when brought to bear on unphilosophical minds, and partly from the speedy prospect of revenge which it held out for the blood of the martyrs sacrificed in the various persecutions. It is difficult to think that but for this latter cause the gentler spirit that ushered in the new religion would have ever degenerated into the ferocious character it assumed under the influence of Tertullian or Augustine. Tertullian, who in one place claims for Christians the sole possession of the virtue of loving their enemies,[2] indulges, at the close of his treatise on the public spectacles, in a foretaste of the joy and

---

[1] *Letter to Demetrianus*, 24. Compare his *Glory of Martyrdom*, 20.
[2] *Ad Scapulam*, 1.

derision that will be shortly afforded him at the Day of Judgment, when he shall behold illustrious monarchs groaning in the lowest darkness with the great Jupiter himself; persecuting provincial governors in fires fiercer than those which, in the days of their pride, they caused to rage against the Christians; philosophers covered with shame as the fire consumes them; charioteers glowing in their chariots of fire; and wrestlers tossing in the fiery billows. These are the spectacles which this great Christian apologist promised to his co-religionists as compensation for the idolatrous spectacles which he earnestly wished them to forgo.[1] It is needless to say that the spirit of fierce, unforgiving vengeance never expressed itself with greater emphasis than in this African Christian's vision of Hell; and it was doubtless this desire and need of vengeance which led to that intensification of future torments which gave so distinctive a feature of terrorism to the new religion, and against which to this day we have still to battle.

When we think of the millions upon millions of our race for whom the joys of life have been embittered, and the physical pains of whose last hours or years have been intensified a thousandfold by the prospect of those coming torments which they were led to regard as the just merits of their sins, at the hands of a God as loving as He was omnipotent, we

[1] *De Spectaculis*, 30.

shall better appreciate that degradation from its original purity which Christianity underwent at the hands of the Church Fathers, who threw philosophy and common sense to the winds, to revel in conceptions as impious as they were coarse; and when we compare their teaching on that point with the beauty and simplicity of the Religion of Philosophy, the religion of Seneca and Cicero, which, irrespective of any certain reward or retribution beyond the grave, could yet teach men to live each day as if their last,[1] and could bid all men to depart from life with equanimity, assured that death either put an end to all evil or was the portal to a happier state, we shall be inclined to call in question the commonly received opinion that Christianity added perceptibly to the happiness or mental progress of the human race, and we shall be tempted to wish either to liberate that religion from the deadly stain of its superstitious accretion, or to restate and re-assert the claims of human reason as they were stated and asserted by Philosophy more than two thousand years ago.

And since they are still legion who insist on the literal and everlasting Hell-fire as the essential doctrine of Christianity, presuming therewith on the innocence of children or the ignorance of the uneducated, it is worth while to trace to its source the idea of posthumous punishment in a subterranean

---

[1] Seneca, *Epist.* 12, and Aurelius, vii. 69.

world, so as to account for its presence, not only in pre-Christian Paganism, but in modern extra-Christian barbarism. In comparative mythology, as revealed in the fancies of common folk-lore, we shall succeed in finding the explanation.

The custom that still survives in Bavaria of speaking of the sun and moon as *Frau Sonne* and *Herr Mond*, and the tale which in the same district accounts for their celestial movements by their relationship as man and wife, carry us back to a time when, as is still attested of several modern savage races, men could think of the two great luminaries as actual human persons of one gender or the other. The human attributes ascribed to them account for the worship that came to be paid to them, often with so much cruelty, in so many parts of the world, belief in their humanity being a natural and almost necessary preliminary to the belief in their divinity. The stories, so numerous in European folk-lore, of the sun or moon taking persons up to themselves as a punishment, as in the *Edda* the moon takes up two children for merely carrying water-pots on their shoulders, point equally to the old state of thought which regarded them as actual living human beings, and to the beginning of the later conception of them, as places rather than as persons.

For just as in Greek mythology Hades and Orcus from being persons became places; just as

Hel, the Norse goddess of death, who received the departed below, gradually lost her personality and became the receptacle of the dead, the place where they were punished; so the Sun and Moon from being persons able to punish, became the places where men were punished, as in the case of the man eternally visible in the moon for gathering sticks on the Sabbath or for working in his vineyard by moonlight. In Swabia one may still hear it said against the practice of spinning or sewing in the moonlight, "Leave off working, or you will go to the moon"; and it is still a common German formula for the asseveration of innocence to exclaim, "May I go to the moon if I did it." The idea is clearly apparent that the moon is a place of punishment; and in accordance with this, in the folk-lore of countries like Russia and North Germany, where cold is more dreaded than heat, the moon figures as the place for future punishment, in the case at least of Sabbath-breakers. With this we may connect the fact that in Norse mythology Niflheim, where Hel received the dead, was imagined to be a world of cold that lay to the north, whilst over against it to the south lay a world of heat; which two worlds we may respectively identify with the moon and the sun, and thence infer, that as Niflheim, the place of future punishment by cold, was in northern climates suggested by the icy cold associated with the moon, so in hotter regions the sun gave birth to the idea of a world where excess of fire and heat would form the basis of future penal suffering for the wicked. And according as either luminary suggested an intensification of the heat or cold, endured in this world, as the probable punishment of the next, so would the other luminary come naturally to be thought of as reversing those conditions, and therefore as a place of sensational delight, reserved only, like the Elysium of the Greeks, or the Indian's happy hunting-grounds, for those who by their bravery or other virtues might be so fortunate as to deserve it.

The one obvious difficulty in the way of this speculation affords really the strongest proof in its favour: namely, that places of future purgatory are invariably subterranean, whereas the sun and moon are aerial bodies. For when we consider that the sun and moon are both seen to rise apparently out of, and again to sink into the earth or sea, and that in the state of thought prior to the conception of space round and below the earth their reappearance is obviously suggestive of a journey under and through the earth during their absence from sight, we see at once that they would themselves be the first cause of the ideas of a subterranean world at all, such as we find in the Egyptian Book of the Dead, where departed souls descend with the Sun-god through the western gate and traverse with him the infernal regions; whilst it would only be natural that the ideas of punishment, originally associated with the sun and moon, would in time become attached to that more mysterious, because unseen, world through which they were thought to travel, and with which existing tradition still connects them in popular tales. To that subterranean world would no less naturally become attached another attribute of future suffering, over and above the fire or frost derived from the sun or moon, namely, its eternity of duration, an idea easily suggested by the unceasing regularity of the solar and lunar movements, and still preserved in European myths, which insist on the everlastingness of the punishment of the unfortunate sinner whose presence and fate is writ large in the moon as an eternal warning to mankind.

It is curious to think that on so childish a conception of primitive thought as this supposed frequent visit of the sun or moon to an underground world has been reared the most terrific superstition which has ever weighed upon the human mind; a superstition which has probably done more to promote human misery than all other evils combined; but a superstition which will not survive the day when for men to simulate assent to doctrines they disbelieve, and to teach as true such doctrines to others, is seen to be as fatally at variance with the simplest postulates of truth and honesty as it is indefensible on the ground of expediency.

CHAPTER VII

THE END OF THE WORLD

As early as the sixth century before Christ, Heraclitus, the famous philosopher of Ephesus, who traced the origin of all nature to fire, speculated also on its periodical reconsumption by the same element; and this idea was afterwards generally adopted by the Stoics, though some of them, like Panaetius and Posidonius, believing that matter itself was from everlasting, believed consistently in the world's eternal duration. The Stoics thought, says Cicero, " that at the end the whole world would be burned, when, after the loss of all moisture, neither the earth would admit of nourishment nor the air of water, the very existence of the latter being rendered impossible by the exhaustion of all water; so that nothing would be left but fire; and that God again giving life to this, the world would be renewed and refurnished as it was before.[1]

[1] *De Natura Deorum*, ii. 46.

So familiar to the world was this notion of the destruction of the earth by fire that Berosus the Babylonian historian, in the fourth century before Christ, even went so far as to predict the actual date of the final conflagration.[1] Seneca, although he seems to have hesitated between a final cataclysm by a conflagration or by a deluge, entertained so little doubt of a violent end to the world, that he used as a consolation under bereavement the consideration that neither the earth, nor the sky, nor the universe, though under the direct guidance of God, were exempt from ultimate destruction.[2] "At that time," he says, "the tides will be released from their bounds. How, you ask? Just in the same way as the future conflagration. Either will happen when it pleases God that the better order of things shall begin and the old order finish. Water and fire rule all earthly things. From these is their beginning, and from these their end. Therefore, when the new state of things is to begin, the sea will be poured down upon us from above just as heat and fire will be when another mode of destruction is chosen."[3]

In another place he describes how at the last deluge all the race of men and animals will be destroyed, and then, when the waters have subsided, every animal will be reproduced after its kind, and

[1] Seneca, *Quaest. Nat.* iii. 28. [2] *Epist.* 71,
[3] *Quaest. Nat.* iii. 28.

man occupy the earth again for a season, innocent of crime and born under happier auspices.[1]

In his letter to Marcia, after describing how stars will fall on stars, and the earth burn with ardent heat, he expresses the belief that at the time of that great convulsion, the human race, as blessed spirits and destined to immortality (*felices animae et aeterna sortiti*), will, when it seems good to God, be restored again to life.[2]

The interest of these ideas is, that the belief in the final triumph of good over evil at the close of the present dispensation of things, together with the belief in the simultaneous resurrection of the dead and the renovation of nature, were among the main tenets of the Persian Zoroastrian religion and of the Jewish expectation of the Messiah; a proof not only of the great interchange of thought between Greece, Italy, and the East in the pre-Christian period, but of the borrowed nature of those early Christian notions concerning the millennium and the end of the world which constituted so strongly marked a feature in the earlier literature of the Church, and so fundamental an article of her original creed.

With regard to the final conflagration of the world there was little if any difference between the Christian and the Pagan belief. It was a belief that sprang naturally from the imperfect knowledge of

[1] *Quaest. Nat.* iii. 30.   [2] 26.

nature possessed by the world at that time, a belief to which modern science lends no countenance whatever, associating fire, as it does, with the beginning rather than the end of planetary life, and deducing millions of years to come from the evidences, derived from astronomy and geology, of millions of years in the past history of our globe. But whereas the Pagan or the Stoic only contemplated the physical destruction of the earth, with the Jew, and consequently with the Christian, a political aspect added itself from the first to the physical speculation of that catastrophe, till at last the end of the world came to mean primarily the political termination of the Roman Empire and the transfer of supreme power from the West to the East. It will appear from the sequel with what tremendous consequences to the destinies of civilisation this physical speculation was fraught.

The time of the origin of Christianity was marked by a state of great mental fermentation, the political agitation of centuries having reduced multitudes, especially in the East, to a condition bordering on actual craziness; and from the political anarchy of the time sprang hopes, and from hopes prophecies, of a mighty deliverer who should end the existing dispensation of things, shake off the dominion of Rome, and vest in the East itself the imperial sceptre of the world. Other nationalities besides the

Jewish indulged in the same dream, and that the expectation was well known to the Roman world is proved by its mention by both Tacitus and Suetonius. "An old and fixed opinion," says the latter, "had prevailed through the whole East, to the effect that it was fated that at that time men from Judaea (*Judaea profecti*) should gain supreme power, and a prophecy which, as the event showed, referred to the Roman emperor, the Jews applied to themselves, and rose in rebellion." It was the general Pagan belief that this prophecy was fulfilled in the person of Vespasian, who was proclaimed emperor during his command of the campaign in Judaea. "Many were persuaded," says Tacitus, "from the ancient books of the priests, that it was indicated that at that very time the East should wax strong, and men from Judaea should gain supreme power: which ambiguities predicted Vespasian and Titus." Even Josephus, who as a Jew must have been well versed in the Jewish prophecies purporting to relate to the Messiah, only spoke of it in the following cold terms: "What chiefly encouraged them (the Jews) to the war (with the Romans) was an ambiguous oracle found also in their sacred writings that about this time some one from their country should obtain the empire of the world. This they understood to belong to themselves, and many of the wise men were mistaken in their judgment about it, for the oracle intended the government of Vespasian, who was proclaimed emperor in Judaea."

It is passing strange that Josephus should have spoken in this way if the educated Jews generally had entertained that expectation of the Messiah which later Christian criticism has always based on certain passages of Moses and the prophets. Evidently Josephus and some of the learned Jews did not interpret those passages as justifying the belief in a coming Liberator. But the belief was common, if it was not universal, among the Jews. In the days of the expected Messiah the righteous were to be raised from the dead and clothed again with flesh : an idea derived apparently from the Zoroastrian religion of Persia, of which it was one of the tenets, that in the end the Good Principle of Light, Ormuzd, should prevail over Ahrimam, the Bad Principle of Darkness; that he should then summon the children of light from their graves, remove all evil from the face of nature, and establish definitely the kingdom of the righteous and of virtue upon earth. It is far more probable that these ideas, which subsequently governed the Christian dogma of the millennium, were derived by the prophet Daniel and the Jews from Zoroaster and the Persians than from Daniel by Zoroaster;[1] but, be that as it

[1] The best modern Parsi researches place Zoroaster's date as far back at least as 1300 B.C. The later date of 521 B.C. arose

may, it would seem that, after the Roman conquest of Judaea, the expectation of the Messiah who was to raise the righteous from the dead and establish their supremacy assumed a stronger political tinge, and passed into the expectation of a Messiah who was not only to be the great Liberator of the nation from the Roman rule, but to establish a great Jewish empire, with Jerusalem for the capital of the world.[1] The early Christians, who inherited the general system of Jewish beliefs, inherited of course this one; and the confused Jewish idea of the final triumph of righteousness and of a temporal kingdom passed with no essential change of any sort into the creed of the primitive Church.

The Roman conquest of Judaea by Pompey (74 B.C.) gave of course new life and meaning to this tradition of a Liberator which the Jews adopted from Persia. Josephus tells of numerous false prophets who, before the final revolt, claimed to be the Messiah with a mission from God to deliver the people from the Romans, and who offered to authenticate their mission by the performance of signs and wonders in the wilderness. Even after the disastrous revolt, due to this expectation, had resulted in the destruction of Jerusalem and the dispersion

from a slight mistake of about eight centuries; a king Gushtasp, in whose reign Zoroaster lived, having been wrongly identified with Darius Hystaspes!—Framji Karika's *Parsis*, ii. 148.

[1] Edersheim's *Life and Times of Jesus*, ii. 431-452.

of the people, a certain weaver called Jonathan again induced a number of the poorer Jews to follow him into the wilderness by the promise of signs and wonders, so strong was the faith of the people in their ultimate delivery.

We are bound to remember this obstinate belief of the Jews, if we would understand the attitude of the Pagans towards the Christians, who to all outward appearance were no more than a sect of the Jews. How could the Christians but inherit the hatred felt for the Jews, when they adhered above all things to that expectation of a temporal kingdom which, based as it was on the anticipated ruin of Rome, was so particularly offensive in the case of the Jews? Looking back, as we can, through the ages, it is easy to see that the Jews misinterpreted their Scriptures in their expectation of a temporal kingdom; but the early Christians misinterpreted them no less, for they expected the immediate return of Christ, and looked forward to a temporal kingdom, and to the overthrow of the powers then in existence. The current idea of the physical destruction and renovation of the world mingled with their expectation of a political revolution, and the dread of the end of all things was surpassed by their hope of a somewhat sensual millennium. Of the early Christians of any distinction, Irenaeus, Tertullian, Lactantius, Papias, Justin Martyr, Montanus, and Cerinthus were all fervent millennarians. The resurrection of the elect from the dead to spend one thousand years in a restored and beautified Jerusalem was Justin Martyr's conception of the orthodox Christian belief of his time. "We confess," wrote Tertullian, "that a kingdom is promised to us upon the earth, though, by heaven, only in another state of existence, forasmuch as it will be after the resurrection for one thousand years, in the divinely built city of Jerusalem let down from heaven." The Montanists, that wild Phrygian sect which Tertullian joined, had a prophecy which foretold the previous manifestation of this very city for a sign; and Tertullian actually believed that this prophecy had been fulfilled during the expedition of the Emperor Severus against the Parthians, when in Judaea every day for forty days was seen suspended in the sky a city which vanished regularly as the day advanced![1]

The Persian ideas of the abundance of renovated nature mixed themselves strangely with the reign of the righteous upon earth under the new dispensation expected by the Church. Paradise itself is a word of Persian origin, and thoroughly Persian was the Christian anticipation of it. Irenaeus, when describing the resurrection of the dead, the reign of the righteous, and the new powers of nature, traces back

[1] *Against Marcion*, iii. 24.

to elders who were personally acquainted with St. John the assurance that the days were coming when vines should have ten thousand branches, each branch ten thousand twigs, each twig ten thousand shoots, each shoot ten thousand clusters, and each cluster ten thousand grapes; and when, if any saint were about to pick one of the clusters, another would cry out amidst the profusion, "Take me, I am a better cluster."

These despicable ideas are only worth noticing for their almost absolute identity with those entertained by the Jews at the same period. The Jew looked for the entire rebuilding of the sacred city of Jerusalem, when it should have become the capital of the whole world in that empire of the Messiah which was to be raised on the ruins of the empire of Rome. The city itself was to be raised to a height of nine miles, and extend from Joppa to Damascus. It was to be as large as Palestine, and Palestine was to be as large as the world. Its windows and gates were to be of precious stones, its walls of silver and gold, and the jewels strewed in its streets every Jew would be free to gather. In those days not only would peace and holiness reign, but the wheat would grow as high as palm trees on the mountains, every tree bear fruit daily, and all sickness and disease pass away. To attempt to formulate any definite system of these wild ideas connected with the coming of the Messiah and the end of the world would be manifestly hopeless; all that can be proved is the extreme similarity between the Jewish and the Christian notions on the subject, and of both with the Zoroastrian notions, —a similarity which, as between the Jews and Christians, touches actual identity only on the all-important point of the impending downfall of the Roman Empire.

As with the Jews, so with, the Christians, the political aspect of the kingdom of the righteous gradually superseded the physical and spiritual aspect, which had been the primary one in the primitive Zoroastrian system. The second coming was expected from year to year, if not from day to day, and the prospect of speedy redress emboldened the Christians to mix denunciations and menaces freely with their predictions of their approaching triumph. Did it embolden a fanatical handful of them to set fire to Rome in the year 64 during the reign of Nero? An affirmative answer is certainly suggested by the language of Tacitus, who appears to have had no doubt of their guilt in connection with that famous conflagration, though he condemned the excessive and extraordinary cruelty of their punishment.[1] At all events, from that time forth the breach was widened between the Chris-

[1] *Annals*, xv. 44.

tians and the Roman authorities ; and the revolt of the Jews two years after the burning of Rome must have further confirmed the latter in their belief of the disloyalty of a body of men who were only regarded as Jewish sectaries. The result was, that the end of the world became more closely than ever identified with the end of the Roman Empire, as in the Apocalypse attributed to St. John or to Cerinthus ; and a few references to the Fathers will prove beyond all doubt how by the early Church the one consummation was as little doubted as the other was eagerly desired.

Tertullian explains the passage, "That day shall not come unless first there be a falling away," as an allusion to the end of the Roman Empire ; and on the words, "He who now hinders must hinder until he be taken out of the way," his comment is, "What obstacle is this but the Roman State, the falling away of which, by being scattered into ten kingdoms, shall introduce Antichrist?"[1] Irenaeus also refers to the allusion in the Apocalypse to the ten kings, who would arise in the last times, and among whom the empire then ruling the earth would be partitioned.[2] And Jerome, in reference to Daniel's vision of the four beasts, says distinctly : "Let us say what all ecclesiastical writers have handed down : At the end of the world, when the kingdom

---

[1] *Resurrection of the Flesh*, 24.   [2] *Against Heresies*, v. 26.

of the Romans is to be destroyed, there will be ten kings, who will divide the Roman world among themselves."

In the condition of the Roman Empire, with its different provinces in constant revolt, and the supreme office of the State at the mercy of the military, the prediction of the dissolution of the political edifice was amply justified by its extreme probability; but to expect that the men who had reared that edifice, and did their best to conserve it, should listen patiently to the Christian anticipations of its speedy disintegration, and of the substitution of ten separate kingdoms for the unity of the empire, is to expect of them not only indifference to their own immediate interests, but disregard for the obvious advantage of the world. The destruction of contemporary civilisation by fire and blood, as foretold in one of the visions of Hermas, in a work originally as well accredited as any of the existing New Testament Canon, or as prophesied in some of those *Sibylline Oracles* which were forged in the supposed interests of Christianity, and are quoted by most of the early Fathers, notably by Lactantius, without the least suspicion, as of equal authority with the Gospels themselves, cannot have conduced to a more charitable consideration of the Church on the part of those who had everything to lose by the fulfilment of the prophecy. No term of insult was too gross for the Christians to apply to Imperial Rome. They habitually spoke of her, in a literature of foolish visions scattered broadcast over the empire, as Babylon, the Harlot, or the Beast, and they omitted no imaginary evil from the pictures they drew of her impending ruin. Of the wildly comminatory and insolent nature of this literature we may form some idea from the still extant Book of Enoch, the Fourth Book of Ezra, the so-called Sibylline Oracles, and the Testament of the Twelve Patriarchs; and from these we may judge of the purport of such lost apocryphal works as the Apocalypses of Elijah, of Zephaniah, of Zechariah, of Abraham, of Moses, of St. Peter, of St. Paul, of St. Thomas, and of St. Stephen. The age of the Antonines was particularly rich in these forged prophetical writings predicting the end of the empire; and every impartial mind must admit not only that the Pagans must have been more than men to have borne these menaces with patience, but that the Roman magistrates would have been political imbeciles had they looked on nascent Christianity, formed largely of Jews in the different cities of the empire, as other than a hostile political force, and an association or conspiracy of more than usual danger to the State.

The prediction of the end of the Roman Empire would naturally commend itself to more than one subject nationality ; and Christianity, falling in with a widespread longing for successful revolt, would flourish with the extension of the hopes it encouraged. There was likely to be no part of the world where, on the terms of a great political revolution, the Christians might not hope to make converts. Predictions of the ruin of the empire had an obvious tendency to self-fulfilment ; and it is remarkable that the invasion of the barbarians and the virtual downfall of the empire in the fifth century occurred at about the time when, according to the computation of an absurd chronology, it was prophesied to take place. The Christians adopted from the first the Jewish notion that the world would end after as many thousand years as it had taken days to be created. "In six days," said Irenaeus, "created things were completed; it is evident therefore that they will come to an end in the 6000th year." This triumph of reasoning was generally accepted as conclusive by the Church, and if other Christians agreed with Julius Africanus that 5531 years had elapsed between the creation of the world and the birth of Christ, the year 469 must clearly have been the year of the anticipated final catastrophe. But allowing for variations of chronological calculation, it must have been expected about the time when under Alaric, Attila, and the rest, the Roman Empire came virtually to an end. We may perhaps never know how far this coincidence was accidental, but the Christianity of Alaric and his invading Goths is a proof of the signal efficacy with which the Church had trained the enemies and ultimate conquerors of Imperial Rome.

If we thus suppose that the political hope of the Church became to a great extent her aim, that from passive contemplation of the end of the Roman Empire she passed to active promotion of the same, and that by so doing she responded to a general desire for political autonomy permeating the provinces of the Roman Empire, we explain in a very natural way much that is otherwise mysterious or inexplicable. We have here, in other words, the main key, first, to the extremely rapid propagation of Christianity; secondly, to the cruel persecution of it by a power previously noted for its usual broad toleration; and lastly, to the ultimate downfall of the Roman Empire, and to its partition, as predicted, among the previously subject nationalities. Without denying that for all these facts there were many other contributory causes, we may well account the political aspiration the primary cause of all, the overruling factor in the historical problem of the early centuries of our era.

Against this theory must be set the fact that Pliny in his famous letter to Trajan makes no direct allusion to the charge of disloyalty against the

Christians, and that similar lack of testimony marks the brief references to them of other Pagan writers like Tacitus and Suetonius. Perhaps in those early days the anti-imperial tendency of the new movement was less apparent or more carefully concealed than it was in later times when the Christians had become a powerful association, ramifying through the whole empire and powerfully organised; but even in Pliny's day sacrifice in honour of the emperor was one of the three tests in the trial of Christians, and it had been precisely this refusal to offer sacrifice for the Roman Empire in the person of the emperor which, according to Josephus, had been one of the immediate causes of the Jewish and Roman war. Eleazar, the son of the high priest, then governor, persuaded the Jewish priests to refuse the gift or sacrifice of a foreigner; and this was the origin of the war with the Romans, for they rejected the sacrifice of Caesar.[1] The Christians, originally identified as they were with the Jews, naturally shared the suspicion of disaffection which attached to the Jews; and so they were called upon to exculpate themselves in the same way, as in the story of the martyrdom of Polycarp, when the authorities, striving their utmost to save him, entreated him to swear by Caesar's Fortune, and asked what harm it could do him to say, Lord Caesar, and to sacrifice. It was the

[1] *Jewish War*, ii. 17.

Christians' disloyalty that was suspected; and if their religion was hated and persecuted, it was more on account of their obstinate refusal to dissociate it from the Jewish taint of disaffection than of any essential doctrine contained in the religion itself. It must too be admitted that their motives for not conforming to the usual oaths of loyalty were often of the most superstitious kind. They had no scruples, according to Tertullian, in swearing by the Safety of Caesar; but to swear by his Fortune or his Genius was impossible, because on the one hand fortune was an unreal and fickle thing, and therefore an oath by it was a light and vain oath, whilst on the other hand a genius was a demon, and an oath by a demon was a wicked oath. Surely there was some excuse for the Pagans if they failed to understand these superfine distinctions and objections, and attributed to downright disloyalty what was really an absurd superstition!

The very fact of the frequent occurrence of pleas in the Christian apologies against the charge of disloyalty proves at least the general Pagan belief in the truth of the charge, for people never defend themselves against accusations that are not propounded. "We pray also for the emperors," said Tertullian, "for their ministers and powers, for the stability of things (*pro statu seculi*), for tranquillity, and for the postponement of the end (*pro mora finis*)"; or again:

"We offer sacrifice for the health of the emperor, but to our God and his, and, as God has commanded us, by prayer alone. For God, the Creator of the universe, needs not the savour nor the blood of anything." Justin Martyr, with less vehemence but equal earnestness, protested against the idea that the Christians were looking for a temporal kingdom; but in another treatise he admitted that he himself and many, though not all, of his co-religionists expected the rebuilding of a beautified Jerusalem and the reign therein of the righteous for 1000 years.[1] This expectation could only have come about by a tremendous political convulsion, so far as the non-Christian could understand it, nor was there anything in the Christian apologies at all calculated to reassure him, whilst the literature that was not apologetic but claimed to be apocalyptic contained everything that was calculated to alarm him.

The simple rite of sacrifice on behalf of the emperor and of respect for the national gods would have removed the suspicion of treason; and the Pagan, accustomed himself to take a part in such rites as the mere forms of the State service involving no necessary assent to the polytheism presupposed in them, was at least excusable if he interpreted the conscientious objection of the Christian to idolatry as the transparent pretext and proof of participation

[1] *Dialogue with Trypho*, 80, 81.

in a treasonable conspiracy. Even if the Christians prayed, as Tertullian declares, for the postponement of the end, the mere expectation of that end, which meant above all things the end of the empire, must have been difficult enough to distinguish from the actual hope of it, which they were at so little pains to conceal, and which was the one point of the new religion whereon there was something like unanimity of opinion amongst its votaries. We must remember that it was not merely the empire, the political edifice, which the Christians opposed, but the whole state of the civilisation of their day. As Vopiscus, a heathen historian of the fourth century, remarked, the Christians made themselves conspicuous for the extraordinary license with which they criticised and condemned the times they lived in; and that at a period when their own lives, as painted by their own writers like Salvian or Cyprian, offered so very little justification for self-gratulation in the matter of superiority of morals.[1]

If we regard, then, the spread of Christianity as to a great extent a political movement looked upon by the authorities as a treasonable conspiracy against the empire, it is no longer unintelligible why the mere name of Christian, apart from any proved criminality, came to be treated as punishable, and why the mere renunciation of Christianity became a

[1] Compare with Salvian, Cyprian, *De Lapsis*, 5, 6.

passport of impunity. This could not have been the case, had they been seriously accused of those crimes of infant sacrifice and nocturnal debauchery with which the popular imagination often charged them. Nor could it have been the case, had their primary offence been their disbelief in the popular gods and the neglect of sacrifice, for a similar atheism on the part of the Stoics and Pythagoreans had long been patiently tolerated. But if the renunciation of Christianity was the equivalent of returning to the ways of good citizenship, of disavowing sympathy with those denunciations of wild revenge, or belief in those prophecies of the impending ruin of the empire which accompanied the spreading faith into the farthest corners of the Roman dominions, this anomaly of judicial procedure admits of explanation. It is otherwise incredible that the Romans, who in their rule over subject nations had so well learnt and practised religious toleration that the friends of toleration have ever since appealed to their example as the golden rule, and who bore in Judaea or Persia with precisely the same dislike of polytheism and idolatry that afterwards characterised the Christians, should have suddenly developed a taste for religious persecution for its own sake, and exhibited the abnormal cruelty which, even if we could suppose that such tales as the martyrdom of Polycarp and of the Christians at Lyons were forgeries palmed upon

Eusebius, still clings to their historical dealings with the Church of the first three centuries. This is the fact that requires explanation, and no explanation meets it so well as the theory that the primary offence of the Christians was less the novelty of their religious doctrines than the disaffection involved in their political opinions.

CHAPTER VIII

PAGAN PHILOSOPHY

ONE of the commonest traditions that has acquired some semblance of truth by persistent reiteration is that the pre-Christian religions at their best had little to do with or little power to enforce morality, and that the conversion to Christianity effected no less a moral than a theological revolution in human society. But if the theory of a theological revolution fails to survive an inquiry into the mass of theological thought which, whether we call it Orientalism, Gnosticism, or Platonism, was prevalent over the whole world from the Ganges to the Tiber at the birth of Christianity, and out of which the evolution of Christian theology is easily traceable, still less will the theory of a great moral revolution survive an impartial inquiry into the higher religious teaching of Philosophy with regard to virtue when the Christians began to take that teaching out of its hands.

The early converts to Christianity forsook no doubt many of the vices of their Pagan state, and became better men than many who remained unconverted; there is no reason to doubt on this point the testimony of their own apologists. The immediate expectation of the Judgment Day, with its tremendous menaces or promises, cannot have been without effect in restraining from vice or in promoting virtue; and the moral conversion so caused was doubtless of equal value with that which often followed lectures on Philosophy or initiation into the mysteries of Isis or of Mithra. But there is no evidence that it was of much higher value; though this proposition needs some justification in the face of the high moral excellence that ecclesiastical writers of all times have claimed for the primitive Church.

We have of course Pliny's evidence that the Christians of Bithynia bound themselves by oath not to commit theft, robbery, adultery, or breach of trust; we have the reluctant admission of Julian that in their care for the poor the Christians set an example to their Pagan contemporaries; and there is other abundant proof that great numbers of them were distinguished by the sincerest philanthropy and a strong desire for the moral and social improvement of society. All this may and must be admitted ungrudgingly. But there is a reverse side to the picture, and a side which, in justice to the Pagan opposition, it is only fair to recollect.

The appalling depravity which St. Paul rebuked in the Corinthian Church proves that some other motive than the pure love of virtue must have attracted men to the new religion; and if that motive was the expectation of a political Eastern Empire, founded on the ruins of the Roman power, the otherwise inexplicable presence in the Church, at the earliest date of her history, of a set of men whose lives were a discredit and a scandal, not merely to the Christian brotherhood, but to civilised Pagan society, admits of explanation. The humane and laudable charity displayed from the first by the Church to the worst of sinners, a charity which is said to have been shown to Constantine when the heathen priests had pronounced the murder of his son Priscus an inexpiable sin, must have tended of itself to give a bad moral complexion to the Church in the eyes of the outer world, even if we take no account of the probably numerous cases of relapse into sin and crime. Antinomianism, moreover, or the doctrine that a state of spiritual perfection exempted men from the obligations of the moral law, and that it was lawful to sin that grace might abound, undoubtedly produced in the early Church the same revelling in sin that the same doctrine produced afterwards among the Anabaptists. Only by these considerations is it at all possible to account for the failure of the educated Pagans to be struck by the asserted high moral excellence of the early Church. Christianity had been some time before the world before the reign of Marcus Aurelius, yet what impressed him about the Christians was not their virtue so much as their obstinacy.[1] Pliny only saw in them a bad and excessive superstition; Tacitus the same; Suetonius the same.[2] Yet unless these men were demented, they must have had some justification, not merely for their blindness to the merits of the Christians, but for their positive bad opinion of them; and that this justification lay in the conduct and character of at least a large minority of the Christians themselves is practically admitted by Tertullian, for this is how he meets the Pagan reproach of moral depravity: "As for your saying that we are a most shameful set, steeped in luxury, avarice, and depravity, we will not deny it is true of some, but it cannot be said of all, not even of a majority of us."[3] A defence surely so faint as almost to amount to a plea of guilty! Only a bare majority of Christians who were not morally depraved!

Tertullian's evidence is supplemented by Cyprian, who lived about fifty years later. Cyprian distinctly gives it as his opinion that the Decian persecution had been amply deserved by the Christians on account of their sins. His description of the Church is as bad as possible. Each man thought only of in-

---

[1] xi. 3.
[2] *Nero*, 16: genus hominum, superstitionis novae et maleficae.
[3] *Ad Nationes*, 5.

creasing his property; among the priests there was no devotion, among the ministers no sound faith; in their works there was no mercy, in their manners no discipline; false swearing, evil-speaking, and quarrelling were rife; many bishops became secular agents, and left their flocks in order to seek merchandise abroad, and were eager in the pursuit of hoarding money.[1]

The interest of this evidence is that it applies to the third century. In the fifth and subsequent centuries, of course, the awful pictures of the state of Christianity by Christian writers like Salvian or Chrysostom leave not a point of advantage on the side of the Church as against the Paganism of any period; but it would seem that moral corruption set in much earlier than is usually supposed, and a description of the Christians by the Sophist Aristides, in corroboration of Tertullian and Cyprian, shows at all events in what moral light they presented themselves to the judgment of contemporary Paganism. Aristides describes them as praising but not practising virtue; as insatiable and avaricious, calling indigence communion, singularity philosophy, and poverty contempt of riches; as making great pretensions to humanity but benefiting no one; as travelling to the ends of the earth to gain rich men; as dexterous at disturbing the peace of families and obtaining control of their affairs; as never saying nor doing any good

[1] *On the Lapsed*, 5, 6.

thing, neither promoting the welfare of cities, nor contributing to festivals, nor comforting the afflicted, nor reconciling those at variance. Then we must remember that the immoral rites with which the Pagans charged the Christians as a body, the Christian sects charged one another with, nor is it fair to expect that the Pagans should have distinguished from the general Christian body the sectarian followers of Carpocrates, Basilides, or Montanus. On the whole the evidence seems conclusive that from the very first the lives of a large minority of the Christians were so bad as fully to justify educated Pagans in their suspicion and dislike of the whole body; and we must consign to the limbo of historical mythology the old ecclesiastical tradition that there was a period of the Church's history when she was not only beyond reproach, but when she held aloft in a depraved world the beacon of a higher morality. If she did so, it would be interesting to know both the date and the place.

It is worth while, in support of this conclusion, to adduce some evidence to show that on all the essentials of virtue and morality the Church taught nothing that had not been taught for centuries before her existence, because so many of the historians of early Christianity are apt, in speaking of the influence of Philosophy at that time, to confer on it at best their contemptuous approval, as an influence of no wide nor deep operation in the world, and as altogether inferior in kind to that of the new religion. This they have done generally from a studied abstinence from the few remaining works of the philosophers, often from sheer indifference to them, and to some extent from a misunderstanding of the different meaning and scope of Philosophy in ancient and modern times. Philosophy nowadays is in common use confined to metaphysics and logic, and is supposed to represent speculative and recondite opinions concerning the universe and all the manifold mysteries of existence. But formerly it meant this and much more; it covered the whole ground now covered by Religion, and consisted not only of speculations about the world and life, but of a code of moral rules reaching to the minutest details of conduct. It represented mental and spiritual cultivation, as when Cicero called it "the culture" or "the medicine of the soul,"[1] or when Plutarch spoke of it as the one remedy for the diseases of the soul. "Let no one delay," said Epicurus, "to study philosophy while he is young, and when he is old, let him not become weary of it; for no man can ever find the time unsuitable or too late to study the health of his soul." This, the spiritual health of the soul, was its primary concern.

Its function was to educate men first to the right

[1] *Tusc. Quaest.* ii. 5, cultura animi ; iii. 3, medicina animi.

worship of the gods, and secondly, to right conduct towards men. According to Seneca, its function was to teach us to obey God, to follow Him, and to submit to Fortune;[1] its light shone not for the few, but for all men, without distinction of persons, inasmuch as a good conscience lay within the reach of all men;[2] if we owed gratitude to the gods for our lives, we owed it to Philosophy for the possibility of living well, for it led us to the truth concerning divine and human things; and, inseparable as it was from Religion, Justice, and Piety, it taught us to worship the gods and to love mankind.[3]

Philosophy covered not only the whole ground now covered by Religion, but the whole ground now covered by Morality. According to Plutarch, it taught us not merely to distinguish between the just and the unjust, the honest and the dishonest, but to conduct ourselves properly to the gods, to our parents, to our elders, to the laws, to strangers, to governors, to our friends, to our wives, to our children, to our slaves.[4]

Moral progress was the object set up by Philosophy as the great aim of life. Men sought after it with a zeal which the Christians, if they rivalled, never surpassed. It was taught at all the schools of Philosophy as well as in the public schools scattered over the whole empire, wherein Philosophy was an

[1] *Epist.* 16. [2] *Ib.* 44. [3] *Ib.* 90.
[4] *Training of Children*, 10.

essential part of the curriculum. The lecturers dealt, like the preachers after them, with such familiar themes as Anger, Superstition, Quarrelling, or Love, and it was open to any man to frequent any discourse likely to be applicable to his own particular case. Plutarch's exhortation to the hearers of such lectures to examine themselves afterwards, and see whether their affections were moderated, their afflictions lightened, their constancy confirmed, or their souls stirred effectually to virtue and goodness, is a strong indication of the extent to which Philosophy controlled and coloured men's lives in those days, doing for them, in fact, exactly what the pulpit or the confessional has done since.[1] Philosophy indeed was everywhere, not only in the schools and public lecture-rooms, but in the palaces of the rich, where it conferred spiritual guidance and training of the heart and head, and in the market-place or forum, or wherever else it could reach the crowd. We hear, for instance, of Apollonius of Tyana addressing crowds in the porch of the Temple at Olympia on Fortitude, Wisdom, Temperance, and other virtues. Philosophy, in short, had not merely its preachers, but its missionaries,—men like Apollonius and Dion Chrysostom, who, shrinking from no danger nor labour, visited all the cities of the empire, preaching, rebuking, reforming,—missionaries whose travels, whose perils, and

[1] *On Hearing*, 8, 12.

whose energy recall and help to explain those of St. Paul and the Apostles.

The letters of Seneca to Lucilius afford a good example of the moral advancement which the votaries of philosophy sought to attain by that medium of communication. Seneca bids his friend to persevere in that which was his sole pursuit—the study of becoming better day by day;[1] he advises him to keep before his mind the thought of some good man, and so to act as if always in his presence;[2] to have for his intimates men who are capable of improving him or of being improved by him;[3] and he reminds him that those must fall back who do not continue to advance, and that retrogression is the inevitable consequence of a relaxation of moral effort.[4] Yet are we not constantly told that in the days of Seneca philosophy was altogether powerless for good?

In the same spirit Epictetus taught that, impossible as it was to be without fault, it was possible to direct our efforts to the attainment of faultlessness.[5] Certain signs, he thought, indicated a man in a state of progress: for instance, that he should blame, accuse, or praise nobody; that he should say nothing about himself; that he should secretly despise praise bestowed upon himself; that if censured he should make no defence; that he should free himself from

[1] *Epist.* 5, 6, and 50. [2] *Ib.* 11. [3] *Ib.* 7. [4] *Ib.* 71.
[5] *Discourses*, iv. 12.

desires; that he should not care whether others thought him wise or foolish; and that he should keep watch upon himself as upon an enemy lying in ambush.[1]

From the task of Self-improvement that of Self-examination is inseparable; and accordingly we find that this latter was a regular practice with the followers of Philosophy. Jamblichus assures us that it was a practice of the Pythagoreans to form resolutions for the day in the morning, and to compare performance with promise in the evening. The Stoics laid special stress upon this habit. It was the wont of the Stoic Sextius, on retiring to rest for the night, to make daily inquiry of his soul of what evil it had cured itself during the day, what vice it had resisted, or in what respect it had become better. Seneca describes how every night his wife would keep a respectful silence whilst he looked back upon the whole of the past day, and reconsidered his deeds and words, hiding nothing from himself, and passing over nothing. He strongly advocated this daily compelling of the soul to give an account of itself: " Anger will cease or become more moderate which knows it will have daily to come before a judge. What then more beautiful than this habit of beating out a whole day? What a sleep is that which follows such an examination! How tranquil and profound and free when the soul has been either

[1] *Manual*, 48.

commended or admonished!" Plutarch also urged no less strongly the duty of constant self-examination.[1]

No Christian writer therefore surpassed the philosophers on the value to be set upon an upright conscience. "You ask," says Seneca, "what the real good is, and whence it comes? It comes from a good conscience, from honest purposes, from upright actions, from a contempt for things of accident, from a placid and constant course of life evenly conducted."[2] "Let us give that peace to our soul which the constant meditation of wholesome precepts will give, and good actions, and a mind only desirous of what is honourable. Let conscience be satisfied. Let us not labour for reputation, or let even bad reputation follow us, provided we really deserve well."[3] He would have a man, falsely accused of ingratitude, be content with the voice of his own conscience, which in the face of a vast crowd of dissentients counts not the number of votes, but triumphs in its own verdict.[4] "My own conscience," said Cicero, "is of more importance to me than what men say." And long before Cicero, Isocrates urged Demonicus not to hope to hide any shameful action, for though he might hide it from others, his own conscience would be aware of it (σεαυτῷ συνειδήσεις).

Sometimes the conscience was identified with that

[1] *Inquisitiveness*, 1.   [2] *Epist.* 23.
[3] *De Ira*, iii. 41.   [4] *De Benef.* iv. 21.

deity or demon within each man's breast which he held as a gift from, and as a living portion of, the Deity, to guide and guard him through life. In this sense, in which it is so often used by Epictetus and Aurelius, the conscience was the same as the guardian angel which would ultimately lead the soul to judgment after death. Therefore it was the Pagan long before it was the Christian ideal "to have a conscience void of offence before God." "What use is it," says Seneca, "to hide oneself and avoid the eyes and ears of man? A good conscience challenges a crowd, a bad one even in solitude is anxious and alarmed. If your actions are honourable, let all men know; if they are disgraceful, what does it matter, if you know yourself? O wretched man that you are, if you despise this last witness."[1] "We should live as if we were living in public, and should think as if some one could see into our inmost heart. And so some one can. For what does it profit that a thing is hid from man? nothing is hid from God."[2] "Let no one think he gains, if nobody shall be aware of his crime. For He knows all things, in whose sight we live; nor if we can conceal it from all men, can we do so from God, from whom nothing can be hidden or secret."[3]

A fine passage on the same subject is attributed to Apollonius of Tyana: "If the soul chooses virtue

[1] *Epist.* 43. [2] *Ib.* 83. [3] Lactantius, of Seneca, vi. 24.

for its object, conscience attends the possessor with pleasure into temples and streets and sacred groves and busy haunts of men. She forsakes him not in his sleep, but bids a chorus of dreams to join in sweetest harmony of song around him. If the state of the mind inclines to do wrong, conscience suffers not the culprit to look fixedly on men, nor to address them with unfaltering tongue. She will not suffer him to approach the temples nor to offer up his prayers in them. She restrains him from raising his hands to the images of the gods." [1]

The logical corollary of this doctrine of conscience was that sin was its own chief punishment, and that no further terrors were really necessary for the enforcement of morality. "The first and greatest punishment of sinners is to have sinned," wrote Seneca, who argued that no wickedness, however prosperous, went unpunished, since the penalty of wickedness lay in the wickedness itself, and the fear of detection was only a secondary penalty.[2] "As Zeus has ordained, so act," said Epictetus, "otherwise you will be punished and injured. What will be the injury? Nothing else than not having done your duty. You will lose your character as a faithful, reverent, and well-conducted man. Do not look for greater injuries than these." [3]

---

[1] Philostratus, *Life of Apollonius*, vii. 14. [2] *Epist.* 97.
[3] *Discourses*, iii.

And as sin was thus its own punishment, so virtue on the other hand was held out as its own reward. Cicero says finely : "All actions seem to me more praiseworthy which are done without ostentation and without the witness of the people. . . . There is no greater theatre for virtue than the conscience."[1] So too Seneca: "The reward (*pretium*) of all the virtues lies in themselves, for they are not practised for remuneration (*praemium*), the profit (*merces*) of having acted rightly is to have acted so"; and he thought that no one set a higher value on virtue than the man who would even lose the character of a good man rather than lose the self-consciousness of his own goodness.[2] In pursuit of virtue no sacrifices could be too great. Wherever it called or sent one, virtue must be followed, regardless of all advantages or the loss of private fortune. Her commands were never to be declined, though obedience should be at the cost of life. "What shall I gain, you say, if I do this thing bravely or that readily? To have done it, I reply; no further promise is held out to you."[3]

Surely there is nothing contemptible in this Philosophy, for all Tertullian's insolent sneers at the philosophers as "animals of some considerable wisdom." It is hard to see for what reasons Seneca should have become a disciple of St. Paul, or what ethical truths he could have learnt from him. It is a common

[1] *Tusc. Quaest.* ii. 26.   [2] *Epist.* 81.   [3] *De Benef.* iv. 1.

assertion that Philosophy was only for the few; wherein lies at least this much of truth, that a system which held up the pursuit of virtue as its own reward could not hope to compete numerically with the disciples of the teaching of Lactantius, that virtue without the reward of everlasting life were a foolish desire.[1] But Philosophy addressed itself to the many, and many were its converts; above all it taught that virtue was attainable by all the world. That deplorable conception of goodness as something altogether extraneous to a man, and dependent rather on grace, election, or sudden conversion, than on his own efforts, a conception which has cost the world so dear in bitter and imbecile contention, was of course altogether alien to the ethics of Paganism. Virtue, argued Seneca, was not the gift of nature, for to become good was an art and required discipline and education, but if we were born without it, we were born for it;[2] nor were any debarred from its attainment, for it was not only the wise man's single real possession, but it was the one thing that lay open to all alike; the one thing that welcomed all men, invited all men, whether freeborn, freedmen, slaves, kings, or exiles; and that, indifferent to lineage or wealth, asked only for the man himself.[3]

Not only was virtue thus held out as within the range of all men, but as attainable without im-

[1] *Divine Institutes*, vi. 8.   [2] *Epist.* 90.   [3] *De Constantia*, v.

moderate difficulty: "There is no vice which cannot be eradicated; the ills we suffer from are curable, and Nature herself, who produced us for good, helps us if we desire to improve. Nor, as some have thought, is the road hard and difficult; the approach to it is on the level ... easy is the way to a happy life, only begin it under good auspices and with the power of the gods." [1]

Such teaching, it is here contended, is far better calculated to promote the cause of virtue than that which came into vogue with those who claimed to be the interpreters of Christianity, and who were never wearied of dwelling on the proneness of man's heart to evil continually and on the hard and narrow way. The Pagan's ethical system was in every respect the better for not regarding men as born in sin nor as the children of wrath. Standing entirely aloof and apart from the beliefs or superstitions of the Jews, it knew nothing of the supposed fall of man nor of original sin, but it regarded man always and everywhere as the child of divine love and solicitude. "You are wrong," says Seneca, "if you think our vices are born with us; they are aftergrowths. . . . Nature accommodates us to no vice, but brings us forth pure and free." [2] Epictetus assumes that we are by nature of noble origin, and that we are constituted by nature to do good, to work for others,

[1] *De Ira*, v. 13.   [2] *Epist*. 94.

and to wish them well. Indeed, the mere fact of man's human nature is throughout classical literature used as in itself the strongest incentive to virtue, instead of, as in the hands of the Fathers, a reason for discouragement or for grovelling moral abasement. Which of these two ways of regarding it is better fitted to have an ennobling effect on character may be judged by comparing the Stoics, who were the products of the one, with the monks, who were the products of the other. The monkish ideal is sufficiently well known; the resolutions which Seneca attributes to the perfect Stoic may well serve to assist the comparison.

" I will look," he is supposed to say, "on death with the same countenance I hear it spoken of; I will obey whatever labours shall come. . . . I will despise riches, whether present or absent. . . . I will be sensible neither of the approach nor of the departure of fortune. I will so live as if I knew myself born for others, and I will thank Nature on this account, for how could she better have provided for my welfare than in giving me to the service of all, and all to my service ? . . . I will do nothing for opinion's sake, all for conscience' sake. Whatever I do, I will do as if all men beheld me. . . . I will be pleasant to my friends, to my enemies gentle and conciliatory. I will pardon before I am prayed to do so, I will anticipate fair entreaties. I will know that the world is my country, and the gods its rulers, and that they stand above and about me, the judges of my acts and words. And whenever Nature shall reclaim, or Reason dismiss my spirit, I will depart with the testimony of having loved a good conscience, and good pursuits, and of having diminished no one's liberty, least of all mine own."[1]

This then presents us with the real picture of Philosophy, not that philosophy, falsely so called, of the later Platonists, wherein magic and superstition abounded, but of Philosophy as seen in its best light and at its best period; and when we look at its ideal with minds free from the traditional contempt cast upon it by its enemies, we at once see that it aimed at a character which combined all the best features of the Christian ideal. In regard to resignation, unselfishness, public spirit, a forgiving and tolerant spirit, the ideally perfect Pagan had nothing to learn from the Christian of the highest type, whilst words fail to measure his superiority to the Christian of the monkish type, with his purely selfish asceticism, his anthropomorphic theism, his ridiculous dread of demons and hell. And how great was Philosophy as a reforming influence, how second to no other in its power to reclaim the individual from sin! Who can suppose that the story of Polemon,

[1] *De Vita Beata*, 20.

the young profligate, who went to scoff at a lecture of Xenocrates, and hearing him discourse on temperance, became then and there a convert to better courses, was unique in the history of Philosophy? Or what Christian can forget that it was to Philosophy, as represented by the *Hortensius* of Cicero, that one of the greatest Christians of his own or any age, Augustine, owed his reclamation from a life of disgusting debauchery and his awakening to the claims of intellectual interests? Truly Apollonius of Tyana uttered a good word when, in answer to the question whether there was anything greater in the world than the Colossus at Rhodes, he replied: "A man, whose whole mind is devoted to Philosophy"; and Cicero expressed the sentiment of a liberal age when he said that one day spent well and in accordance with Philosophy was preferable to an eternity of error.

With the closing of the schools of Philosophy at Athens by Justinian, Philosophy, degenerate as it in many respects had become from its earlier state, ceased to operate as a moral influence over the lives of men; and human reason was given over entirely to the uncontrolled tyranny of priests and monks and to the wasting debility of insoluble theological discussions. If, as Gibbon says, Plato would have blushed to acknowledge those who last bore his name and supported his opinions, what would he have thought, could he have foreseen that centuries after his death the sole or the chief intellectual human interest would centre in the monophysite or monothelite controversy? Fortunately for him he was spared the prophetic vision of the coming glacial period of human intelligence, of the time when men would account monasticism, as Chrysostom accounted it, the only true philosophy. And fortunately for us, that glacial period has begun to pass away, and already there are signs that Philosophy may again come to occupy her place as of old, may again, in the wreck of the superstitions and ignorance that have passed over her like a flood, rise to her legitimate place of power and influence, and, when men know not whither to turn for guidance and consolation, may reconduct them to the principles of a rational piety and to the simple rules of a sound morality.

CHAPTER IX

PAGAN MORALITY

HAVING given some idea of the general moral teaching of Paganism, and of the higher ethical principles of Philosophy, it remains to make the picture more complete by going so far into detail as to examine some of the ideas of pre-Christian or Pagan writers with regard to self-sacrifice, charity, toleration, liberality, forgiveness. These virtues are those which have ever been specially inculcated and illustrated by Christianity, not of course in its history, but in the private life of individuals, or at least of its higher representatives; and if a comparison between the Christian and Pagan ideals of virtue be instituted on these aspects of conduct, at least the ground will not have been chosen which *primâ facie* is to the advantage of Paganism.

1. It may be said, however, to begin with, that the duty of self-sacrifice, the duty of the individual to merge all private or selfish interests in the wider

interests of his community, was the first principle of all political life in antiquity. The whole history of Athens, Sparta, or Rome, is nothing else than the illustration of that principle in practice; and the idea of, no less than the word, "devotion" is of Pagan Roman, not of Christian Roman origin. Still it is claimed that the idea of the moral beauty of self-sacrifice did not illuminate the world before the Christian era; and therefore it is desirable that Philosophy should speak for herself in a matter whereon her shortcomings have so often been held up to reproach.

To live as if he knew himself born for others has already been alluded to as one of the characteristics in Seneca's picture of the ideal Stoic; and his other references to the subject deserve attention. "It is required of a man to be of benefit to men, to many if he can, failing that to a few, failing that to those nearest him, failing that to himself."[1] "No man can live happily who regards himself alone, who turns everything to his own advantage; it behoves you to live for another, if you would live for yourself."[2] And, comparing the Stoic with the Epicurean view of happiness, he says: "Our pleasure is to benefit others, even at our own labour, provided we lighten the labours of others; or at our own peril, provided we save others from peril; or at our own

[1] *De Otio*, 30. [2] *Epist.* 48.

loss of fortune, provided we alleviate the necessities and distresses of others."[1] "See the force of what is honourable : it will lead you to die for the commonwealth, even though you shall have to do so at the very moment you know it must be done. Sometimes from a very beautiful deed a great joy is derived in the shortest moment of time, and albeit no advantage from it shall reach its doer after death and his removal from earthly interests, nevertheless the mere contemplation of the deed he is about to do delights him, and the brave and just man, when he places before himself the rewards of his death, the liberty of his country, the safety of all, for which he sacrifices his life, is in the highest state of happiness and derives enjoyment from his personal peril."[2] All this in the supposed degenerate days of the early Roman Empire!

How different from Tertullian who, pouring contempt on the old sentiment of its being a man's duty to live for his country, empire, and state, declares that none is born for another, because he is destined to die for himself alone![3]

Aurelius, too, never wearies of reminding himself that man is by nature a rational and social animal, whose function and true work is to labour for his fellow-man, his fellow-kinsman, as the child of the same God. It is utterly false to say that this idea

[1] *De Benef.* iv. 13. [2] *Epist.* 76. [3] *Ascetic's Mantle,* 5.

of the brotherhood of all men rests on the teaching of Christianity. It was one of the dominant ideas of Philosophy, especially of Stoicism, long before the foundations of the Church were laid. Marcus Aurelius rises from the conception of the political community to that of the wider community of humanity with a breadth of spirit that at no time of her history has belonged to the Church, regarding as she ever has done all who are ignorant of or indifferent to her teaching as aliens and enemies and outcasts.

"The whole world is in a manner a state," he concludes; and "my city and country as far as I am Antoninus is Rome, but so far as I am a man it is the world. The things then which are useful to these cities are alone useful to me." The idea of humanity as a whole, of all mankind as one fraternity, independent of all barriers of race or language, was first grasped by the philosophers; the hold of it was rather relaxed than tightened by the Church; and the narrow nationalism of modern Europe contrasts poorly with the cosmopolitanism of the pre-Christian world. The supreme pontiff of Pagan Rome offered up prayers for the whole human race. We have the testimony of Plutarch that the Pagan priests prayed not only for whole communities, but for the whole state of mankind.[1] It was Cicero,

[1] *Philosophers conversing with great men*, 3.

and no Christian, who said : " Nature ordains that a man should wish the good of every man whoever he may be, and for this very reason, that he is a man." [1] When Socrates was asked to what city he belonged, he answered, " To the World " ; nor was his conception of moral duty as conterminous with humanity ever afterwards lost. It was upheld by Diogenes the Cynic, as by Zeno the Stoic. Seneca only professed an axiom of philosophy when he wrote : " We ought to devote our soul to no particular place. This is the conviction with which we must each live : I was not born for one corner, my country is this whole world." [2] Plutarch, speaking of the lost work of Zeno, called the *Republic*, says : " The much-admired *Republic* of Zeno aimed singly at this, that neither in cities nor towns we should live under distinct laws one from another, but should look on all men as our fellow-countrymen and citizens, observing one manner of life and kind of order, like a flock feeding together with equal rights in a common pasture." [3]

Moreover, this conception of human brotherhood was distinctly based on the prior conception of the relation of the sonship of all men to God, through participation in His reason. Hear Epictetus : " Never, in reply to the question to what country

---

[1] *De Officiis*, iii. 6.   [2] *Epist.* 27.
[3] *The Fortune of Alexander*, 6.

you belong, say you are an Athenian or a Corinthian, but that you are a Cosmopolitan (κόσμιος). . . . Why should not a man call himself a citizen of the world, why not a son of God, when he has intelligently observed the government of the world, and learned that the greatest and highest and broadest community is that composed of men and God, and that from God have descended the seeds not only to my father and grandfather, but to all beings generated on earth, and particularly to rational beings, who alone by their nature have communion with God?"[1]

Nor were these principles confined to the lecture-room or the cabinet. They bore magnificent fruit in that conception of a law of nature, applicable to all classes and nations of men, upon which the whole later system of Roman law was founded. How different the tendency and result of Catholicism, which has ever withdrawn men from the ties of family and country, not to the service of humanity at large, but to the servitude of the Church! and whose votaries, in ceasing to be patriots, have become not cosmopolitans but sectarians, with no broader horizon for their sympathies or affections than that of their creed and their sect! Of all the historical conventional myths still current in the world there is none with so little foundation in fact as that of a broad Christian spirit of unity, or of a

[1] *Discourses*, i. 9.

world-embracing Christian charity. That idea of the brotherhood of mankind was an idea which, as it had its origin from Philosophy, so perished with Philosophy; nor has the history of the Church from the time of its conquest under Constantine onwards for more than a millennium been anything else but the history of cruelties, riots, wars, and persecutions, the horror of which in its entirety the human mind is incompetent to grasp, but the like of which may be searched for in vain in the pre-Christian annals of the world.

2. The duty of charity was of course involved in the doctrine of humanity, nor did the Church ever inculcate it with more earnestness than writers like Seneca. It is necessary to prove this, in order that the following description of Pagan society may be judged at its proper value: "The instinctive impulse of the human heart prompted men to isolated acts of kindness, and even the more deliberate practice of benevolence is recommended by many of the philosophers. But it is recommended on selfish grounds."[1] Why then did Seneca write: "This is the mark of a great and good mind, to aim, not at any fruit from its kind deeds (*beneficiorum*) but at the kind deeds themselves. . . . Virtue consists in conferring benefits not as destined to return, benefits the fruit of which the good man reaps at

[1] Croslegh, *Christianity judged by its Fruits*, 67.

the moment of conferring them."[1] Considerations of gratitude were to be absent from charity; and Seneca would have a man imitate in that respect the gods, who bestowed their gifts even on men who ignored their existence, or accused them of neglect, injustice, or idleness; and who yet, like the best of parents, smiling at the rude speeches of their little ones, ceased not to heap up benefits on those who doubted the existence of the giver. "Let us be like them, let us give, though we give much in vain."[2]

Lactantius does not scruple to claim for Christianity the teaching of the duty of benevolence for its own sake, and to charge Cicero with advocating the practice of liberality only towards persons who can give something in return. Cicero indeed advocates discriminate charity as against indiscriminate, by which many had ruined themselves, but on behalf of deserving persons, not, as Lactantius implies (by mistranslating *idoneis hominibus*), of persons suitable because able to make a return. He also advocates the virtue of charity entirely on its own merits, without any reference to ulterior benefits.[3]

The more common misstatement is that charity was an unknown virtue altogether before the Church taught it to the world. Here again it is unnecessary

---

[1] *De Benef.* i. 1.   [2] *Ib.* vii. 31.
[3] Lactantius, vi. 11, and Cicero, *De Officiis*, ii. 85.

to do more than translate a few passages from Seneca. "Here is another question. How are we to deal with men? . . . What commands do we give? To spare human blood? A fine thing not to injure him whom it is your duty to benefit! Highly laudable forsooth for a man to be gentle to man! Nay, but we will further bid him to stretch out his hand to the shipwrecked, to show the erring their way, to divide his bread with the hungry. But why should I enumerate all that he must do or avoid doing, when I can shortly give him this formula of human duty: all this that you see, the world of gods and men, is one; we are members of a great body. Nature brought us forth as relations when she produced us from the same beginnings and for the same ends. She it is that inspired us with mutual love and made us sociable creatures. She it is that ordained what is fair and just. It is from her ordering that it is more miserable to injure than to be injured, from her command that helping hands are prepared."[1]

Nor was this duty of charity confined to narrow bounds, for the Pagan was taught to help also his enemy. The Stoics said: "To the very end of life we will be in action, we will not cease to labour for the common weal, to help individuals, to give aid even to our enemies" (*inimicis*).[2]

[1] Seneca, *De Otio*, 28.   [2] *Ib.*

Where again, in what may be called the etiquette of charity, will you find greater tact than in Seneca's discrimination between the benefits to be conferred with publicity and those which secrecy should accompany? Military rewards and honours and whatever gifts are enhanced by their publicity should be publicly given, but gifts which confer no honour, but are simply in succour to infirmity, poverty, or shame, should be given silently, with no other witness than the giver and the recipient. Sometimes even the latter should be deceived, so as not even to know the name of his benefactor. "It is too little, you say. Too little, if you think to play the usurer, but if you wish to give in the manner most acceptable to the recipient, you will be content with your own testimony. Otherwise it is not the doing of a kind action which delights you, but the fact of its being known. 'I wish him to know,' you say. Then it is a debtor you wish for! 'I wish him to know,' you say. What! even if it be better and more becoming and more pleasant for him not to know!"[1] Surely this is in the spirit of Christianity, even if it is not the old familiar language. At all events it disposes of the idea that benevolence for its own sake was unknown in pre-Christian days. Or if more is wanted, let there be added this from Aurelius: "What more dost thou want when thou hast done a

[1] *De Benef.* ii. 9.

man a service than the fact of having done it? Art thou not content to have done something conformable to thy nature, and dost thou seek to be paid for it, as if the eye demanded a recompense for seeing or the foot for walking?"[1]

But, it may be objected, at least the practice of charity did not equal the theory; and in helping the poor or visiting the sick there is no comparison possible between Pagan and Christian. Yet immediately the stories recur of Cimon the Athenian giving of his abundance to feed the poor and clothe the naked; of the Lacedaemonians supplying the people of Smyrna with food in time of scarcity, and replying, when thanked for it, that they only deprived themselves and their cattle of a dinner; of Apollonius reminding Vespasian that the supply of the needs of the poor was one of the best uses of a sovereign's wealth; of Arcesilaus visiting Apelles, and to relieve him of the indigence to which sickness had reduced him, placing twenty drachms under his pillow, whilst pretending to make him more comfortable; of the Roman nobles, after the accident to the amphitheatre at Fidenae whereby 50,000 persons were killed or wounded, opening their houses and procuring doctors and relief for the victims; of all the cities of Asia relieving with money or shelter the victims of the great earthquake in Smyrna in 177 A.D.[2] Seneca's

[1] ix. 42.   [2] Aristides, i. 260.

description of the wise man offering aid to the shipwrecked, hospitality to the exile, money to the needy, redeeming prisoners from their chains, releasing them from the arena, and giving sepulture to the criminal,[1] is clearly a picture drawn from nature and daily life, not from his imagination; and to suppose that such deeds required the impulse of the Church to make them more common is to suppose that human nature itself changed with the change that came over religion.

But it involves something more than an assumption of extreme intrinsic improbability, and that is a spirit of wanton disregard for the historical evidence which alone is enough to dispel the assumption. For whether we glance at Athenian or Roman society, we may detect a constant solicitude for the welfare of the poor. In the best days of Athens none of her citizens were in want for the necessities of life; for the rich, according to Isocrates, regarding the poverty of their fellow-citizens as a disgrace to themselves and the city, helped all who were in need, sending some abroad as traders, letting lands to others to cultivate at fair rents (ἐπὶ μετρίαις μισθώσεσι), and enabling others to engage in different occupations. The Areopagus too checked pauperism by providing public works.[2] In the same direction operated such customs or institutions as the free

[1] *De Clementia*, ii. 6.   [2] *Areopagiticus*, 12, 21, 38.

schools; the exemption of orphans from the State charges; the maintenance at the public expense of the children of citizens killed in war; the payment from the treasury of a few obols a day to the poor, the wounded, or the incapable; the donation of a portion of the sacrificial victims to the poor; and the repasts set out in the streets by the rich each new moon, nominally in honour of Hecate, but practically for the benefit of the poor.

The objections that economists might urge against the socialist tendency or nature of these measures would apply with tenfold more force to the monthly distributions of corn to the people that became customary in Rome, and after a time, not merely of corn, but of cheese, bacon, oil, and even clothes. But whether these distributions prevented or promoted pauperism, there is no question of the intention. Under Nerva and Trajan the monthly distributions of food became extended to the children of poor families all over Italy; a portion of the interest of money lent by the State to the landlords on mortgage serving to defray the expense. Alexander Severus founded free schools for indigent children. Nerva and Trajan made laws in favour of orphans. Every quarter of Rome had its *archiater*, or paid medical officer, whose function it was to attend on the sick; and a law compelled every one who gave a feast to make some provision first for the poor of his district.

3. From the seventh century before Christ the story of Pittacus, one of the seven wise men, was famous in the Pagan world. When he had it in his power to avenge himself on some one who had wronged him, he let him go, saying, "Forgiveness is better than revenge, for whilst the former is the sign of a gentle nature, revenge is that of a savage one."[1] Nor have the Jews any finer story to tell than the Pagan story of Gescon the Carthaginian, who, having been recalled from exile and made chief general, when his enemies were given over to his revenge, contented himself with treading gently on their prostrate necks, and saying, when he had sent them away, "I have not returned evil for evil but good for evil."[2] When Caesar made an edict to build and restore the statue of his enemy Pompey, Cicero told him that he had erected an everlasting monument in his own honour.

The whole current of Pagan teaching was in unison with these stories, to an extent that has been purposely ignored. When Diogenes was asked how a man might best revenge himself upon his enemies, he replied, "By becoming himself a good and honest man."[3] Epictetus, when consulted as to the best means by which a man might give pain to an enemy, answered, "By preparing to lead himself the best

[1] Epictetus, Frag. 68.   [2] Polyoenus, v. 2.
[3] Plutarch, *On hearing the Poets*, 4.

life he can."[1] The conclusion of Plato was that we should never return injustice for injustice, nor repay with evil the evil done to ourselves.[2] His later disciple, Maximus of Tyre, pleaded for the forgiveness of injuries on the ground that the avenging of them was worse than the original offence.[3] His other disciple, Plutarch, wrote as follows: "It is eminently humane, and a clear sign of a truly generous nature, to bear the affronts of an enemy when you have a fair opportunity to revenge them. For if a man sympathises with his enemy in his affliction, relieves him in his necessities, and is ready to assist his sons and family if they desire it, any one that will not love this man for his compassion, and highly prize him for his charity, must have, as Pindar says, a black heart made of adamant and iron."[4] From Seneca comes: "Some one is angry with you, provoke him in return with kindnesses. . . . Some one has struck you, withdraw; by striking back you will give both an occasion and an excuse for many blows"; or again: "A great mind that truly respects itself does not revenge an injury, because it does not feel it."[5]

All these passages must count for more, as showing the general forgiving spirit of Paganism, than the one bit of bad advice given by Isocrates to Demonicus,

[1] Frag. 130. [2] *Crito*, 49. [3] *Diss.* xviii.
[4] *How to profit by our Enemies*, 9. [5] *De Ira*, ii. 34; iii. 5.

where he says: "Think it equally disgraceful to be surpassed by your enemies in injuries as by your friends in good actions." Isocrates in this instance fell below his ordinary level. He it was, at all events, who advised Nicocles king of Crete so to behave to weaker states than his own as he would wish more powerful states to behave to himself; and who also wrote as one exhortation for Nicocles to make to his subjects: "That which it angers you to suffer from others, that do not to others yourselves."[1]

4. If regarding the virtues of self-sacrifice or attention to duty, of charity or of forgiveness, the Pagans had as much to say, and said it as well, as the Christians, they seem even to have surpassed them in the degree to which they inculcated the humane virtue of toleration and leniency. When we remember the attitude of uncompromising hostility of early Christianity towards Paganism, and then the intense bitterness of its sects towards one another, we shall appreciate the full value of the old tolerant Pagan spirit of gentleness which breathes in almost every line of a treatise like that of Seneca *On Anger*, and of which the following extracts may give some idea. "If we would be fair judges of all things, let us first persuade ourselves of this, that no mortal is without fault. . . . Perhaps you hear that

[1] Nicocles, 13: ἃ πάσχοντες ὑφ' ἑτέρων ὀργίζεσθε ταῦτα τοὺς ἄλλους μὴ ποιεῖτε.

some one has spoken ill of you; think whether you did not so first of him, think of how many you speak so.... The vices of others we have before our eyes, our own behind our backs.... A great part of mankind are angry not with the sin but with the sinners. Looking to ourselves will make us more moderate, if we ask ourselves, Have we never done anything of the kind, have we never erred in like manner?"[1]

"Why should a good man hate sinners when it is error that drives them into wrong? It is not the part of a wise man to hate those that err, else will he be an object of hatred to himself. Let him think how many things he does himself contrary to good conduct, how many of his actions need pardon, then will he be angry with himself. For a just judge passes the same sentence in his own case as in that of others. No one will be found who can acquit himself, and whoever calls himself innocent regards external testimony, not his own conscience. How much more humane it is to show a gentle and paternal mind towards sinners, not to persecute but to recall them. If you meet a man astray in the fields from ignorance of his road, it is better to direct him aright than to drive him away."[2]

"In order not to be angry with individuals, you must forgive the whole world and pardon the human

[1] *De Ira*, ii. 28. [2] *Ib.* i. 14.

race. If you will be angry with young men and old for sinning, you will be angry with children, who will sin in their turn. Yet who is angry with children, whose age precludes them from a just discrimination of things? and yet it is greater and fairer excuse to be a man than to be a child. . . . The wise man will not be angry with sinners. Why? Because he knows that wisdom is not born with a man, but is the product of time. He knows that very few in every age grow to be wise, because he has a clear vision of the conditions of human life. . . . The wise man therefore, lenient and just towards sinners, goes abroad daily with this thought: 'I shall meet many men given over to wine or to their lusts, many ungrateful, many avaricious, many mad with ambition.' All such things he will look upon as kindly as a physician looks upon his patients."[1]

"We are all inconsiderate and improvident, all uncertain, querulous, ambitious. Why hide the common sore with soft words? we are all bad; and whatever fault we find in another each of us will also find in his own breast. Why notice the paleness of this man, or the thinness of that one? It is the general ailment. Therefore let us be more lenient one to another; bad ourselves, we live with the bad. One thing only can make us quiet, a treaty of mutual toleration" (*facilitatis*).[2]

[1] *De Ira*, ii. 10.   [2] *Ib*. iii. 26.

"Let his age be the excuse of a child, her sex of a woman, his liberty of a stranger, his intimacy of a domestic. In this his first offence let us think for how long he has satisfied us. Or has he offended us in other ways? Let us bear with what we have borne for so long. Is he a friend? He did it against his will. Is he an enemy? He but played his part."[1]

In all this we see the Stoic philosophy shorn of the severe austerity with which it was commonly associated, and from which Seneca was at pains to defend it. "I know," he says, "that the sect of the Stoics has a bad reputation among the unlearned as too severe ... for it is objected to it that it denies that the wise man can pity or pardon ... but no sect is more kind or lenient, none more philanthropic and attentive to the common welfare, as having for its aim to be of use and assistance, and to consult the welfare not of itself alone, but of all men collectively and singly."[2] Of course the same spirit corresponds with the better spirit of Christianity. But the important thing to notice is, that the spirit of charity, toleration, and humanity, which is fondly claimed by the Church as her own special product, was really the product of Philosophy, and especially of Stoicism, and that the Church simply claimed for herself what her utter inability to appropriate would

[1] *De Ira*, iii. 24.   [2] *De Clementia*, ii. 5.

alone prove to have been foreign to her. The borrowed plumage of Philosophy never sat well on the ecclesiastics. If you want to find the true spirit of the Founder of Christianity, you will find more of it in the fragmentary literature of Paganism than in all the works of the Fathers put together; and more, not merely of its spirit, but of its actual expression, in Seneca, Plato, Aurelius, or Plutarch, than in Augustine, Jerome, and all their tribe, the difference between the respective histories of the Church and of Philosophy being only too amply reflected in their literature. There is indeed no fact more patent in history than that with the triumph of Christianity under Constantine the older and finer spirit of charity died out of the world, and gave place to an intolerance and bigotry which were its extreme antithesis, and which still unhappily rule in its stead.

It was perhaps owing to some vague sense of this fact that arose the Christian legend of the conversion of Seneca and the fictitious correspondence between him and St. Paul. But the same theory would have to be applied to most of the philosophers, who expressed themselves in precisely the same spirit. Several centuries divided Plutarch from Plato, but the former would still advise people, when inclined to anger with any one, to repeat to themselves the philosopher's question, "Am not I perhaps such an one myself?" His plea for the humane treatment of slaves might still be often urged on behalf of modern servants ; and his confession, that in this department of life the pressure of his wife or friends had too much incited him to anger, is atoned for by the recommendation of the deferring of punishment and of the greater reformative efficacy of pardon. Epictetus too uses Plato's doctrine, that every soul is deprived of truth unwillingly and therefore errs from a wrong opinion, as a motive for a man to be gentle, tolerant, and ready to pardon.[1]

Aurelius constantly refers to the same doctrine for reminding himself of the same rule of conduct. "When offended at another's fault, think in what manner thou dost err thyself. By attending to this thou wilt quickly forget thine anger, if thou considerest this also that the man is compelled."[2] "It is no way right to be offended with men, but it is your duty to care for them and bear with them gently."[3] "Shall any one hate me, let him look to it; but I will be gentle and benevolent towards every man and ready to show even him his mistake."[4] Had these men anything to learn from a Church which counts among her highest products men of such relentless bigotry as Athanasius, Cyril, or Augustine?

[1] *Discourses*, ii. 22.   [2] *Discourses*, x. 30.   [3] ix. 3.
[4] xi. 13; and compare vii. 26, 63 ; ix. 42; x. 436 ; and xi. 18.

CHAPTER X

CHRISTIANITY AND CIVILISATION

A WIDER subject of comparison between Paganism and Christianity now meets us, regarding their respective contributions to the progress of civilisation. How far did Philosophy improve daily life, and how far was it capable of ameliorating the worst customs of Pagan society? At least we need find no difficulty from the meaning of the terms. Each man, of course, has his own ideal of civilisation; but the general use of the term is fair enough which measures it by reference to certain broad and well-defined aspects of life and conduct. If we desire, for instance, to judge of the civilisation of a given nation or epoch, we invariably ask, what is, or was, the character of its domestic life; what its attitude with regard to women, to slaves, to criminals, to animals; or to customs like war or the sacrifice of human victims. Nor is any other method possible, however arbitrary the standard of measurement may seem. Even so restricted, the problem is complicated enough as between Philosophy and the Catholic Church; although the comparison, to be complete, should properly include their respective services to material and mental progress, that is to say, to all arts and inventions on one side, and to science and literature on the other. But on such points as those reserved for comparison, each subject is in itself of such magnitude, that the impossibility of dealing exhaustively with it in a short space makes it necessary to direct our attention solely to certain leading facts and considerations in connection with it rather than to all the evidence which could be brought to bear upon it. We must be content to skim the surface, trusting that even so we may not fail of reaching the real heart of the questions as they arise.

1. First, then, we may ask—

To what extent did the change from Paganism to Christianity affect or improve the ties of domestic life? There are those who point to the changes effected in this direction as the greatest of all; and the low legal status of sons, the degradation of women, and the facility of divorce, in the time of Pagan Rome, constitute apparently impregnable arguments in their favour.

But, happily for humanity, laws are not always a fair index of facts, but possess such a change-resisting force that the practice and life of any people are in general in advance of its legislation. The Roman laws affecting sons tended constantly to improve, and the son's power over property to increase as against his father. But throughout Pagan history a man's duty to his parents ever ranked next to his duty towards the gods. The theory of his whole duty in life was summed up in the exhortation of Isocrates to Demonicus : " Fear the gods, honour your parents, respect your friends, and obey the laws." Epictetus laid it down as a man's duty to take care of his father, to yield to him in all things, and to submit even to his blows or reproaches ; to look upon all he himself possessed as his father's, never to blame him, nor to say nor do anything to injure him.[1] For the purposes of a fair comparison, we must contrast this old-world theory of duty with that which came widely into vogue with the triumph of Catholicism, that a man owed no duty to his father or mother where it conflicted with his private notions of the interests of his own soul or of the Church ; nor is there anything more distressing or repulsive in the annals of the Church than the countless stories, with which the lives of the saints and hermits are full, of their cold-blooded desertion of parent, wife, husband, or child, of their heartless disruption of family ties, of their selfish disregard for the claims of affection. So highly, indeed,

[1] *Discourses*, ii. 9, and *Manual* 30.

did the merit of this course of conduct come to be regarded, so thoroughly did it come to pass current for the highest ideal of virtue, that there is scarcely a life or legend of a saint in which the desertion of his nearest relations is not recorded as one of the leading features of his sanctity, as one of his chief titles to honour.

Many writers seem to imply that family affection of any sort was as foreign to pre-Christian life as a knowledge of modern astronomy; whereas the evidence of all classical literature and of monumental inscriptions suffices to show that in this respect human nature was precisely the same two thousand years ago as it is to-day. The same evidence may be appealed to in disproof of the common assertion of a wide difference between the two periods in the relationship of husband and wife. Let it be granted that divorce became easy, and, in spite of legislative efforts to the contrary, common; let it be admitted that Juvenal reveals some black features in the Pagan society of the time of Trajan; but let the brighter side be also kept in view, if we have any concern for a truthful judgment.

Against the society depicted in the *Satires* of Juvenal must be set the society, or state of society, depicted in the *Letters* of his contemporary Pliny. The two seem to live in and yet to see two wholly different worlds. It is about as reasonable to judge of the age of the Antonines by the sole evidence of a satirist as it would be to judge of our modern life solely by the light of our society journals or the chronicles of our divorce court. The Romans at all events looked back at a period of six hundred years during which there was no recorded case of divorce. In the worst times it was never more than the exception. Plutarch speaks of thousands of men and women who observed an inviolable community of affection and fidelity to their lives' ends. His short work on *Conjugal Precepts* proves not only the mutual affection on which the matrimonial tie was based, but reveals the close similarity both in theory and practice between the marriages of pre-Christian and Christian times. The monumental inscriptions of every period of Paganism, couched in terms of the tenderest affection, and often recording not merely the number of years, but also the number of months, days, or minutes during which the union of life and love lasted, thoroughly endorse the impression conveyed by Plutarch. And Tertullian himself alludes, in a letter written to his wife against the custom of a second marriage, to the numbers of heathen women who devoted an uninterrupted widowhood to their love for their husbands' memory.

2. Considering the very recent abolition of slavery in the colonies of the leading nations of Europe, and

the system of serfage till a few years ago prevalent in Russia, it is easy to press too far the influence of the Church in the movement which ended in this conspicuous triumph of humanity. The opposition of the Church to slavery was always rather fitful than constant. The early Church never called slavery in question at all; the Fathers, in their Hebrew bondage, held it to be amply justified by the legend of the curse of Ham. The Pagan emperors did more to mitigate its abuses than the Christian emperors. The appointment of a magistrate by Nero to hear the complaints of slaves against their masters, in order to restrain the cruelty of the latter and to compel them to give their slaves sufficient maintenance,[1] shows the sensitiveness of the Pagan conscience to the evils of the system, and the determination to remedy them. By a law of Claudius, a master who omitted to tend his slave when sick lost all rights over him. Hadrian took away the master's right of life or death over his slave; the murder of slaves was made punishable by law; private prisons for slaves were suppressed; the Petronian law forbade their exposure to fight with wild beasts. On the other hand, the Christian emperors between Constantine and Justinian did nothing to mitigate the master's right to torture his slave, nor to give legal recognition to slave marriages. Legislation

[1] Seneca, *De Benef.* iii. 22.

returned rather to its old severities. Therefore the inference is a fair one that had Paganism been prolonged, the influence of Philosophy would in eighteen centuries have effected in this respect whatever the Church can claim to have done in that long period of time.

Horrible stories of the old Pagan slave-system abound. Four hundred slaves were executed in accordance with law for a murder committed by one of their number living under the same roof.[1] The Emperor Augustus is said to have had a slave crucified for eating a quail which had never been worsted in a quail-fight. But it is to the credit of the same emperor that, when he was dining with Vedius Pollio, and the latter ordered a slave to be thrown to the lampreys in his fish-pond for the fracture of a crystal vase, he not only had the man set free, but the fish-pond filled up, and all his host's vases broken in his presence.

But Plato's remark, that many a man had found his slaves better in every way than his brothers and sons, and that slaves had often saved their masters' lives and property, reveals the existence of a brighter side even to slavery.[2] There is the story of the slave who in one of the civil wars hid his master, and then personating him by taking his dresses and rings, gave himself up to the other side to be slain.

[1] Tac. *Ann.* xiv. 42.   [2] *Laws*, 776.

When Asinius Pollio promised liberty to the slaves of Padua if they would betray the hiding-place of their masters' arms or money, or of their masters themselves, not one slave was faithless to his trust. When Philip at the siege of Chios invited the slaves to revolt by promising them liberty and their mistresses in marriage, the women and the slaves rushed with one consent to the walls and repulsed the enemy.[1] Against the fact of the Servile war must be fairly set the voluntary offer by the slaves of military service in the second Punic war. Many were the monuments raised by masters to their slaves, or by slaves to their masters, whose mutual affection and gratitude are attested by inscriptions to this day.

The footing between the two classes was one of considerable familiarity. Masters and slaves seem habitually to have had their meals together; and if Cato advised the selling of old slaves, he ate and drank with them himself, and had them tended when ill by his wife. At the Saturnalia masters laid meals for their slaves, and so did the ladies on the first of March.[2] But of course the fashion was neither uniform nor permanent. Seneca praises Lucilius for living on familiar terms with his slaves, and ridicules those who thought it a disgrace to take supper with them. He reminds him that they are men, fellow-

---

[1] Plutarch, *Virtues of Women*, 3.   [2] Macrobius, i. 12.

lodgers, humble friends, and, since fortune is supreme over all conditions, in reality fellow-slaves. He condemns the growing fashion of his time of not allowing them to speak, and declares that the slaves of earlier times, who were free to speak not only before but with their master, were ready to be executed on his behalf, and to turn upon themselves the danger that threatened him: "They talked at meals, but they kept silence at torture." He deprecates the proverb, "So many slaves, so many enemies." If they were enemies, they were of their master's making. And he sums up his precepts, and presumably his own practice, on this subject with these words: "So live with your inferior as you would have your superior to live with you. . . . Live gently and kindly with your slave, and admit him to conversation with you, to council with you, to a share in your meals."[1]

Elsewhere he says: "It is praiseworthy to exercise a moderate mastery over slaves, and we shall think not how much they can be made to suffer with impunity, but how much is allowed by the nature of the Good and Equitable, which bids us even spare captives and men bought for money. . . . If all things are legally permissible against a slave, there are things which the common law of animate life forbids to be done against a man."[2]

It is important to notice that the later Christian

[1] *Epist.* 47.   [2] *De Clementia,* i. 18.

arguments against slavery really originated with the Philosophers, especially with the Stoics. Before the test of virtue there was no distinction of persons, neither bond nor free. Seneca decided that a slave could be a benefactor to his master, "because the question is not of what station the benefactor is, but of what mind: no one is precluded from virtue; it lies open to all, welcomes all, invites all, whether well born, freedmen, slaves, kings, or exiles; is indifferent to family or income, and content with the actual man. . . . A slave can be just and brave and magnanimous, therefore also he can confer a benefit."[1] "It is an error to think that servitude descends into the whole man; the best part of him is exempt. Men's bodies may be subject and assigned to masters, but the mind remains independent. . . . It is the body which fortune gives over to a master,—this he can buy and sell; but that inward part cannot be given in ownership."[2] These and similar arguments contained nothing new. They had been the commonplaces of Philosophy, irrespective of sect, since Socrates. There were many in the days of Aristotle who contended that slavery was contrary to nature, and so iniquitous. It was formally condemned by Zeno, the first Stoic. And even on the stage Euripides, Sophocles, and Menander expressed the same sentiments that have been quoted from Seneca.

[1] *De Benef.* iii. 18. [2] *Ib.* iii. 20.

The conclusion suggested by these facts is, that where Christianity insisted on the better treatment of the slave, as it did of course often in noble language, it only carried on the ideas and movement begun by Philosophy. And making allowance for exceptional instances of barbarous treatment, and remembering the numbers of slaves who not only obtained emancipation but rose to positions of honour, comfort, or even wealth, one cannot but doubt whether a fair comparison between their status and that of servants or day-labourers in modern Europe would result in so positive a verdict in favour of the latter as is commonly believed. It is sufficient to have glanced at the nature of the evidence on either side to perceive that the picture of the Pagan system of slavery as painted by modern Christian writers is far blacker than that evidence would justify, if, instead of being intentionally mutilated, it were given in its entirety.

3. Nothing in Christian Europe but the burnings and tortures of men for their religious opinions can compare for atrocity with the Pagan gladiatorial games. Even if most of the victims were criminals, the institution of the games will ever remain the darkest blot on Paganism, just as their abolition will ever remain one of the brightest records of Christianity. Every one knows the story, from Theodoret, of the monk Telemachus, who travelled

all the way from the East to Rome, and, leaping into the arena to part two gladiators, fell a victim to the fury of the spectators. That was in the year 404, and the Emperor Honorius from that time put a stop by edict to the custom.

But it was only to combats between man and man that the edict can have applied, for the more brutal and cruel combats between men and beasts long survived Telemachus, and one of the laws of this same Honorius provided for the supply of wild animals for the amphitheatre at Constantinople. Salvian, who was presbyter of Marseilles in the fifth century, and who has left a most woeful picture of the moral condition of the whole Christian Church of his time, complains, among other things, of the delight his co-religionists took in seeing their fellowmen torn and devoured by wild beasts in the amphitheatres! He speaks of "numberless thousands of Christians" as daily spectators of the obscenities of the theatres or of the cruelties of the circus! The Church festivals competed in vain with the public games, which constituted the special mode of thanksgiving for prosperity or victory. If this was not the case in all cities, it was due to some obvious reason, but not to the growth of Christian feeling. Thus it was not the case at Metz, for it had been destroyed by the barbarians; nor at Cologne, for it was full of enemies; nor at Trèves, for it had been four times devastated. A similar reason applied to most of the cities of Gaul and Spain; whilst in the Roman towns the cessation of the games was due, not to the increasing humanity, but to the increasing poverty of the times. The low state of the treasury (*calamitas fisci et mendicitas Romani aerarii*) no longer allowed of them. They did not take place in all the cities, because the cities where they used to take place no longer existed. That they were no longer universal was to the credit of the misery of the times, not to that of the Christian discipline (*miseriae est beneficium non disciplinae*).

We have here undoubtedly the real key to the explanation of the gradual abolition of the gladiatorial games in Europe. No doubt the feeling of the better Christians was against them; but that Christians as a body never systematically absented themselves is proved, not only by Salvian, but by the treatise to remonstrate with them for attending them by Tertullian, in which the objection to them is based far less on their cruelty than on their incidental connection with idolatry; by the well-known story in Augustine's *Confessions* of the Christian who went to them at the solicitation of his friends; and by the story of the Christians interrupting Constantine at the celebration of the games with shouts of "One God, one Christ, one bishop!" But the better feeling of the Pagans was against them no less; nor is it possible to believe that the heroic act of Telemachus would have been as successful as it was had not a large force of Pagan opinion coincided with the Christian on the subject.

There is distinct evidence of this Pagan opposition to the games reflected in classical literature. Cicero attests the fact that some of his contemporaries thought them cruel and inhuman, and he implies his own consent to that opinion.[1] The proposal to establish the games at Athens was effectually stopped for some time by the remark of the philosopher Demonax, that before doing so they would have first to overthrow the altar of Pity. Apollonius of Tyana, the Pythagorean, not only openly rebuked the Athenians for the gladiatorial fights, to see which they ran in crowds to the theatre on the Acropolis, but himself refused to go to their assembly as a place polluted with blood. There is no mistake of Seneca's dislike to the games; and he contrasts the early Romans who spared the lives of dumb animals with his own contemporaries, who scrupled not to kill one another, and that not from motives of anger or fear, but merely for a spectacle.[2]

Add to this the laws passed from time to time to check the frequency of the shows or the number of combatants, or such facts as that Nerva prohibited matches and contests of gladiators,[3] and that Marcus

---

[1] *Tusc. Quaest.* ii. 17.   [2] *Epist.* 90 and 7.
[3] Zonaras says: " gladiatorum compositiones et certamina vetuit."

Aurelius compelled them to fight with blunted swords, and it is evident that there must have been a strong current of Pagan feeling against the popular pastime, a current strong enough in itself to have brought it to an end, even though no Christian opposition, or still more, no scarcity of funds, had arisen to promote the process of abolition.

4. But no triumph of civilisation caused by or connècted with Christianity can compare in importance with the abolition of human sacrifice under the influence of Pagan civilisation. Traces of the gradual disappearance of this custom over the world are clearly marked in history long before Christianity, for which Eusebius claimed the credit of its abolition in or about the reign of Hadrian. At one place Diphilus, a king of Cyprus, abolished it, substituting an ox for the human victim. At Heliopolis in Egypt, Amasis abolished it, substituting the sacrifice of three figures of wax. At Carthage, Iphicrates the Athenian abolished it, if on this point we may credit Porphyry. In Italy one tradition was that human sacrifices to Pluto and Saturn had been common, till Hercules came and persuaded the people to offer instead figures in human shape ; whilst another tradition pointed to Junius Brutus, after the expulsion of the Tarquins, instituting the sacrifice of the heads of onions and poppies for those of men and children.[1]

[1] Macrobius, i. 7.

Roman civilisation consistently opposed the custom. It is probable that the decree of the senate, alluded to by Pliny as passed in the year 96 B.C., definitely prohibiting human sacrifices, a custom openly practised to that time,[1] applied to the provinces of the Republic, not to Rome itself; for Livy, referring to the extraordinary sacrifice in the year 216 B.C. of two Gauls and Greeks of either sex, in obedience to the command of the *Sibylline Books*, says that they were buried alive in the cattle-market, a place which had been previously stained with human sacrifices, a rite by no means Roman (*minime Romano sacro*).[2] It seems incredible that this burial of foreigners in the cattle-market can have survived to the time of Pliny, though we have his word for it,[3] in the face of the law of 96. Pliny himself, referring to the steps taken by Tiberius to stop the practice in Gaul, declares it impossible to estimate the debt of the world to the Romans for their efforts to put it down.[4] Thus children were sacrificed to Saturn in Africa, till Tiberius as proconsul hanged the priests on the sacred trees above the temples,[5] and Hadrian prohibited the sacrifice of men to Jupiter in Cyprus.[6]

---

[1] *Hist. Nat.* xxx. 1; "ne homo immolaretur."   [2] xxiii. 57.
[3] *Hist. Nat.* xxviii. 2; and Plut. *Marcellus*, 3. Plutarch refers to certain rites still performed every November in consequence of the human sacrifice at the time of the Gallic war.
[4] *Hist. Nat.* xxx. 1.   [5] Tertullian, *Apol.* 9.
[6] Lactantius, i. 21.

Cicero could scarcely have spoken of the practice as a monstrous one, still disgracing Gaul in his day,[1] unless the sentiment of Roman civilisation had been energetically pronounced and directed against it.

In order to support the claims of the Church in the matter of human sacrifice, stress is generally laid on Pliny's account of superstitious people, who, to cure themselves of epilepsy, were wont to descend into the arena, to drink the blood of the slaughtered gladiators;[2] or on the 300 Perugian captives slain by Octavius on an altar sacred to the deified Julius.[3] The latter case was probably an act of military barbarity cloaking itself under a religious disguise. It rests on the authority of Lampridius that the Emperors Commodus and Heliogabalus indulged in human sacrifice, in connection apparently with the Mithraic religion; but this was a charge habitually made with reference to religions of which the mysteries were little understood. The sacrifice of children was a charge habitually made against the early Christians, not only by the Pagans, but by the Christians against one another; and it was doubtless in the same spirit that the ecclesiastic, Gregory of Nazianzen, declared that the vaults of Julian's palace at Antioch were positively crammed with the

[1] *Pro Fonteio*, 10.   [2] *Hist. Nat.* xxviii. 2.
[3] Suetonius, 15.

bodies of children and virgins sacrificed by the Emperor Julian for purposes of divination.[1]

There remains, however, another case. Lactantius declares that even in his time Jupiter Latiaris was still worshipped by the Latins with human blood.[2] Tertullian says that Jupiter had still blood given to him to taste in Latium;[3] and Minucius Felix speaks of Jupiter Latiaris as still worshipped with the blood of a criminal.[4] The Fathers on this point appear to be corroborated by Porphyry, when he says: "Who does not know of the festival celebrated in the great city in honour of Jupiter Latiaris where a man is sacrificed?"[5] It is difficult, however, to believe that even here more was meant than that a libation of the blood of a gladiator, slain in the arena, was offered to Jupiter; for Dionysius Halicarnassus, who, in writing on the antiquities of Rome, had occasion to make special mention of the annual festival of the Feriae Latinae, refers to nothing more than the offering of lambs, milk, and cheese, and the sacrifice of a bull, in honour of Jupiter Latiaris. We may therefore conclude that in this matter the

[1] *Oratio* i. 92. Mr. King has the following significant note on this passage in his *Julian the Emperor*: "It was a common trick of the monks to hide human bones in temples, and then point them out as evidences of human sacrifice. A notorious example is the Mithraeum at Alexandria. Nothing is more likely than that the same stratagem was practised in Julian's palace at Antioch by some zealot." [2] i. 21. [3] *Scorpiace*, 7. [4] *Octavius*, 30.
[5] *On Abstinence from Animal Flesh*.

repulsive survival of an abominable custom has been exaggerated to mean the actual continuance of that custom itself; and that the real abolition of that custom was due to the progressive civilisation of ancient Rome.

5. With regard to cruelty to animals, the Church has at no time recognised the existence of any moral duties outside the human species. Whatever feeling of that sort has grown up within the last century must be credited to a more humane growth of mind, which is the consequence rather of increased science than of Christian sentiment; and in spite of the enormous cruelty of Pagan society that was involved in the games, it may be doubted whether the culture of the few was not, even in the worst days, as much in advance of the general sentiment as it is in our own times. In none of the Fathers would you be likely to find a sentiment at all approaching to this of Marcus Aurelius : "As for the animals that have no reason . . . since thou hast reason and they have none, make use of them with a generous and liberal spirit." [1]

The ever-humane Plutarch is strong on behalf of the animals. He resents the notion that no justice is due to dumb animals, and insists that if they must be killed to be eaten, they should be killed with sorrow and pity, and not by such torments as were involved in running red-hot spits through pigs,

[1] vi. 23.

or in shutting up cranes or swans to be fatted.[1] He traces elsewhere a connection between human inhumanity and the custom of seeing and taking pleasure in the slaughter of beasts in the chase. He also makes the curious suggestion that one of the reasons for the Roman custom of always letting a candle burn out, instead of extinguishing it, was that fire, being regarded as a kind of animal, men were thence to learn the lesson of not killing any harmless animated creature.[2] He also thinks it easy to show from the writings and religion of the ancients that they thought it sinful to eat or kill a harmless animal, and he ascribes to this motive of justice the abstinence of Pythagoras from fish.[3]

The Pythagorean rules for refraining from certain kinds of food are of course connected commonly with the doctrine of the transmigration of souls, and many at all times have been the jokes about eating a grandparent in eating a bean. But other motives must have operated, for we have it on the authority of Jamblichus, who wrote the *Life of Pythagoras*, as well as on that of Diogenes Laertius, that the Pythagoreans held it wrong to slay or injure animals that were harmless; that for this reason they disapproved of hunting;[4] and that one of the motives Pythagoras had in prohibiting the

---

[1] *On Eating of Flesh.*
[2] *Roman Questions,* 75.
[3] *Sympos.* viii. 8.
[4] *Life of Pythagoras,* 21.

slaughter of animals was that, in consequence of such restraint, men might be more inclined to think it unlawful to slay one another and to engage in war.[1] Consequently the Pythagoreans always opposed animal sacrifice, the tradition being that the only altar at which Pythagoras ever worshipped was the altar at Delos to Apollo the Parent, for the reason that on that altar no animal had ever been sacrificed.[2]

This abhorrence of animal sacrifice was one of the most prominent features in the career of Apollonius of Tyana, the disciple or rival of Pythagoras in the time of Vespasian. But his protest against cruelty is even more remarkable. At Ephesus he endeavoured to turn the people from their cruel sports to intellectual and philosophical studies.[3] And at Babylon, when the King Bardanes invited him to join in a chase of lions, bears, and panthers, in an enclosure reserved for that purpose, Apollonius replied that it would ill become one who had never even been present at sacrifices to lie in ambush in order to see wild beasts put to needless pain.[4] What would he have thought of modern England, where so many still derive their highest pleasure from the pain of defenceless animals?

Nothing was more common in Roman society

---

[1] *Life of Pythagoras*, 30.   [2] Macrobius, *Saturnalia*, iii. 6.
[3] Philostratus, *Life of Apollonius*, iv. 2.   [4] *Ib.* i. 38.

than this point of view, even in the worst days of the amphitheatre. Abstinence from animal food was openly taught and practised for the very same reasons that influence our modern vegetarians. Seneca in his youth was so strongly impressed with the teaching of Sextius, the Stoic, to the effect that man had quite enough food without the shedding of blood, and that the laceration of animals for the service of our pleasures led to habits of cruelty, that he abstained from animal food altogether for a year, and only returned to it to please his father, who, at a time when Tiberius had proscribed all foreign religions, and a vegetable diet seemed to savour of them, entreated his son to discontinue a practice that was fraught with so much danger to his liberty.[1]

The feeling therefore against cruelty to animals came into existence before and independently of Christianity—the feeling which led Cicero to write that it was a wickedness to hurt an animal;[2] nor is there any proof or indication that the Church in the course of her long reign has contributed in the least degree to the strengthening of that honourable feeling.

6. One fair test of civilisation is the relation between crime and punishment; the absence of cruelty in the latter and of torture to detect the

[1] *Epist.* 108.   [2] *Rep.* iii. 8 : Scelus est nocere bestiae.

former. Punishments and tortures in the days of Pagan Rome were of frightful barbarity; though we have the remarkable testimony of Seneca that an increase of cruelty in this respect had followed the increase of the national prosperity. Pompey was the first to cause criminals to fight with elephants in the arena.[1] The civil wars of Marius and Sylla introduced punishments of thitherto unknown savagery.[2] The cross, the fiery tunic, the wooden horse (*eculeus*), and similar penalties came into vogue. But Seneca, representing doubtless in this every school of philosophy, protested constantly and with all his power against this state of things: "Whilst we are among men, let us cultivate humanity; let us not be an object of fear or danger to any man." And his whole theory of penology, expressed with as much lucidity as humanity in his treatises on Anger and on Mercy, was more rational and philanthropic than anything that was written with any effect before Montaigne. It is true that Augustine used the same common-sense arguments against Torture[3] that were first listened to by the rulers of the world when urged by Beccaria fourteen centuries later; but the Church, as a body, never headed the slightest movement against the atrocious system of tortures and punishments which disgraced Europe during all the

[1] *De Brevitate Vitae*, 13.
[2] *De Sen.* iii. 18.   [3] *City of God*, xix. 6.

centuries of her supremacy. The movement in favour of the mitigation of punishments and of the abolition of torture was begun and carried to a successful issue by the French Encyclopaedist school of Voltaire and Diderot and Beccaria, on principles that were simply a return to the principles advocated ages before by Seneca and the Philosophers; and the Church, if of any force at all in the matter, manifested rather open hostility than inert indifference to a reform of permanent importance to the increased happiness of the world.

7. The same has been her attitude with regard to war. Arnobius in the third century boasted that since Christianity had taught men the duty of the non-requital of injuries, wars had diminished in the world;[1] and Eusebius also claimed for the new religion an effect that may be more reasonably ascribed to the military supremacy of the Roman Empire. But it is notorious that many of the Fathers looked on war as unchristian, for its close connection with both idolatry and bloodshed; a feeling which went so far that the early Christians would not even suffer the inscription on their seals of swords or bows.[2] Yet from the days of Constantine to our own what has Christianity as a religion done for the cause of peace on earth? A little during the Middle Ages, but absolutely nothing since

[1] i. 6.   [2] Clemens Alex. *Paidagogus*, iii. 2.

the Reformation. Wars in Europe are as frequent and well-nigh as ferocious now as they ever were in pre-Christian days; and the movement that has risen to make them less frequent and ferocious is distinctly due to philosophers like Voltaire, Bentham, and Kant, and not to the Church in any appreciable degree whatsoever.

But here again Philosophy has simply returned to the point it had reached in the old Pagan days. After an interruption of about fifteen centuries, we are returning to the position and principles of Cicero, Seneca, Plutarch and others. For the Philosophers no less than the Fathers were on the side of peace to a degree that has never been recognised. When Titus had taken Jerusalem and refused the crown offered him by the neighbouring nations, Apollonius of Tyana wrote a letter offering him instead the crown of moderation for refusing to be crowned for a military success and the destruction of his enemies. Celsus, the anti-Christian, disapproved of international wars.[1] Plutarch thought there was nothing more disgusting than the mutual killing of men in war;[2] and he held that Nicias, the Athenian, for his love of peace, must have stood in point of honour above all comparison with Crassus, though the latter should have made the Caspian Sea or the Indian Ocean the boundary of the Roman dominion. Cicero

[1] Origen, *Against Celsus*, iv. 83.   [2] *Contradictions of Stoics*, 33.

deemed it necessary to protest against the common opinion which attached more importance to military than to civil matters; and of the two methods of settling disputes, namely, by argument or by force, he contended that the former method alone was worthy of men, the latter only of wild beasts.[1] Dicaearchus, a disciple of Aristotle, wrote a book, unfortunately lost, on *Human Destruction*, wherein, after estimating the loss of human life by floods, pestilence, devastation, and wild beasts, he showed that more men were destroyed by one another in wars and seditions than by all other causes put together.[2]

Lastly, we come to Seneca, always foremost on the side of humanity. What protest against the war-spirit of his own or later days could have been stronger or truer than the following: "We punish murders and individual homicides; what of wars and the glorious wickedness of slaughtered nations? Neither our avarice nor our cruelty knows a bound. Such crimes when committed secretly or by individuals are less injurious and less appalling; but it is by senatorial decree and the vote of the people that our cruelties are exercised, and what is forbidden in private life is commanded by public ordinance. Actions which, if committed by stealth, would meet with capital punishment, we praise because committed by soldiers. Men, the gentlest species of the

[1] *De Officiis*, i. 11, 22, 23. [2] Cicero, *De Off.* ii. 5.

animal race, are not ashamed to find delight in mutual slaughter, to wage wars, and to transmit them to be waged by their children, when even dumb animals and wild beasts live at peace with one another."[1]

With all this evidence before us of the strong anti-military feeling of the leaders of Pagan thought, —evidence quite as clear as that of the anti-military feeling of the early Christians,—and with the recollection not merely of the little that the Christianity of at least a thousand years has contributed to the cause of peace, but of the number of wars for which the Church herself has been primarily responsible, and of the vigour with which she has almost invariably fanned the war-spirit,—the conclusion must force itself upon every impartial mind, both that the world owes no progress to the influence of the Church in this direction, and that it probably would have owed more to Philosophy, had its beneficent influence prevailed to later times.

Under all the seven foregoing heads therefore it is clear that the debt of civilisation to the Church, indisputable as it is in some respects, is not so great as most Church historians would have us believe. The progress that in certain lines has accompanied Christianity is not necessarily for that reason its consequence ; and the ideas that preceded

[1] *Epist.* 95.

and conditioned such progress were mainly of Pagan, and especially of Stoic, origin. In the eclectic philosophy of Seneca lie the germs of every reform or advance that has occurred since; the feeling against slavery, against cruelty to animals, against cruelty to criminals, against war, was not only openly expressed, but readily and widely received. Whether, if the course of history had been uninterrupted, the arms and philosophy of Rome would have carried civilisation in Europe to its present pitch we can only amuse ourselves by speculating; but there is at least no evidence that it would not have done so, and had there been no invasion by the barbarians, nor overthrow of the Roman Empire, the world would have been spared the fearful history of its Dark and Middle Ages; and the light of the Grecian humanity, instead of having now to be revived, might never have been extinguished.

CONCLUSION

FROM the evidence collected in the preceding chapters, we are now in a position to estimate at their real value the differences between Catholicism and Paganism, and the debt of civilisation to Catholicism as a factor in history. That both those differences and that debt have been unfairly exaggerated by partisan writers is a conclusion supported by a comparison of the ecclesiastical Fathers of the first ages with the Pagan Philosophers who were their contemporaries and often their adversaries; but it may be well to recapitulate briefly the general results of the survey we have concluded.

In the Pagan world the uneducated classes had of course a large numerical preponderance, but so splendid was the system of education in the Roman Empire that the educated minority bore probably a far greater proportion to the majority than, till our own time, has ever been the case in the world. And in this educated class it is easy to discern a general monotheistic belief, underlying all the polytheistic superstructure; for the Christians themselves admitted that the Philosophers taught the unity of God, whilst countenancing the worship of many gods out of deference for human frailty or ancient custom.[1] The rightful attributes of the Supreme Deity, His omnipotence, goodness, and mercy, were no less connected in the civilised world with the names of Zeus or Jupiter than they were or came to be in Palestine with the name of Jehovah. Between the several nations of the earth the main religious difference had become one rather of nomenclature than of fundamental belief; and so little had the Greek or Roman to learn of either the Jew or the Christian on the great problems of Providence or design in nature, that the vast masses of Christian literature subsequently devoted to those subjects contain no arguments that may not still be found in abundance in the fragmentary literature of the pre-Christian classical world.

Still less did Catholicism introduce any change into the Pagan theory of secondary or subordinate divine agencies. Only a change of diction ensued, the word angels or messengers, which had long been in use as a synonym for the gods, coming at last to supersede the latter term altogether. The saints and martyrs displaced the gods and heroes, but the new angel-worship differed to no appreciable degree,

[1] *Clementine Recognitions*, x. 48.

theoretically or practically, from the old polytheism it supplanted.

With the purified and rationalised theology of Paganism co-existed an earnest spirit of religion and devotion, of which the main features were a strong sense of the duty of humble trust and reliance in the goodness of God, of patient resignation to His will, and of spiritual endeavour to approximate His pérfection. Not long ago it was said by Cardinal Manning that the Old World "destroyed man by a distorted theology, a perverted morality, and a deification of human power."[1] But it is time that this Catholic misreading of history received its despatch. It was a primary article of the higher Pagan faith that every man, inasmuch as he shared the spirit of God, might and should consider himself as a Son of God, and that therefore it behoved him to conduct himself in a manner befitting a temple of God, and to regard all his fellowmen as his brethren by virtue of their belonging to the same family with himself. The morality and dignity of daily life flowed to a great extent from this consideration, and the rightful dealing with his fellowman was a religious duty of only secondary importance to a rightful conception of the real attributes of the Deity. That the philosopher Longinian could have written to Augustine that the best way to God was by words and deeds

[1] Sermon in Pro-Cathedral, 11th October 1885.

that were pious, pure, just, chaste, and true, is a proof that the Pagan and Christian ideals of duty coincided more than they differed.

The hope of a future existence encouraged the Pagan to perseverance in well-doing during his life, and the prospect of heaven and immortality presented itself to him as the only possible alternative to the prospect of unending repose in death. Only to the illiterate or the ignorant remained any fear of those everlasting punishments in hell, which, having originated none knew how, added a terror the more to man's natural fear of the cessation of physical consciousness.

The spirit of hostility to superstition was one of the first principles of true philosophy, nor need we turn from Seneca to Tertullian and the Fathers to acquire any fresh or greater contempt for the polytheism, the idolatry, or the love of magic, that were rife among the uneducated classes of the Old World. The Fathers in their fulminations against superstition said nothing that the Philosophers and Poets had not said much better before them. It is possible that among the lower social strata Catholicism spread purer ideas of religion than any that filtered down to them from the upper strata of Paganism; but that the grossly superstitious practices of the Pagan multitude had their full counterpart in the Church itself from the earliest period it would require a bold or an indifferent controversialist to deny. The sensual love-feasts of one place or period, the wild asceticism at another or the same, the idolatrous cult paid to the bones of martyrs and to images, the processions and pilgrimages to shrines, the exorcising of demons, the fraudulent miracles;—these and other practices, still regnant in Catholic countries with a vigour little abated by either the lapse of time or the growth of knowledge, justify the doubt, not only whether superstition, in consequence of the conversion, came to differ much, if at all, either in intensity or volume from the pre-Christian standard, but even whether it underwent much change in its actual outward form. Polytheism changed in expression more than in character. Like the colossal image of Apollo that surmounted the famous image of the first Christian emperor at Constantinople, Paganism continued to retain the topmost place in the system that nominally superseded it.

With regard to special virtues, abundant proof has been adduced that Platonists, Pythagoreans, and Stoics preached and practised the duties of charity, beneficence, toleration, and forgiveness with quite as much earnestness and success as distinguished the Catholics after them. So effectually, indeed, had Philosophy advocated the claims of the great principles of humanity, that in Paganism, before there was any Church at all, there was a party audible in

15

its outspoken opposition to slavery, to cruelty to criminals or to animals, to the gladiatorial games, and to war.

If then between the higher Paganism and the higher Christianity there was so little moral or spiritual difference, how, it may be asked, did Catholicism come to assert itself at all, to say nothing of its rapid and easy conquest of the forces of Philosophy arrayed against it? The answer, forced upon us by so much as is still extant of its apocalyptic literature, is, Because it coincided and co-operated with a long-smouldering political movement against the Roman Empire,—a movement which, unhappily for the world, only too well succeeded, involving, as it did, in the ruin of Rome, the ruin of civilisation, of order, of peace, of prosperity, and above all of sound and simple theological ideas, based on healthy reason and common sense. From this point of view no friend of progress and science, looking back at the consequences of the triumph of Catholicism over Paganism, can fail to regard it as a distinct and immeasurable misfortune to the world; he has only to read side by side with one another the early Christian Fathers and their contemporaries the Pagan Philosophers to perceive that the inferiority of the former to the latter reaches not merely to the language and style but to the reasoning and moral sentiment; and he will fervently regret that the long contest between Hellenic and Judaic thought ended so completely in the victory of the latter.

In the pre-Christian world there was evil enough, revealed on many a black page of history, but its better aspects are no less impressive, and equally claim our recognition. To ignore them purposely is to sin against historical truth, without really advancing the cause of Christianity. But in addition to the justice of bringing this better side into prominence, the field we have traversed opens up vistas of no small speculative interest. The truths of religion are eternal, but not the dogmas of theology; and if, as other theologies have passed before it, Catholicism is destined to pass in its turn, a rational curiosity may well lead us to wonder what will be the faith that will come one day to rule in its stead. Historical and literary criticism, and above all the growth of more scientific and entirely new ideas both of man's place in the world and of the world's place in the universe, have sapped and are still sapping the intellectual bases of the Church, causing secessions that are none the less real for their not being overt or declared. A silent but far-reaching transformation, very different from the violent Reformation of three centuries ago, is taking place before our eyes and all are asking: What will be its result? In the early days of the struggle of the Church with polytheism her adversaries complained, with every appearance of justice, that many were driven to the extremes of irreligion and immorality through the overthrow of their belief in the ancestral gods; and who will say that the intellectual revulsion of our own epoch threatens us with no similar danger? Is there no probability that with thousands the loss of their faith will prove at the same time the loss of their restraints from vice no less than of their incentives to virtue?

If this danger is not an imaginary one, how to meet it becomes a question of the highest practical importance. Our sacerdotalists would have us seek a remedy from the malady itself, by returning to that very Catholic tradition which has been the main source of the evil. Others think we may find a substitute in esoteric Buddhism, in Indian theosophies, or even in the so-called manifestations of spiritualism. But has not the religion of Philosophy —a religion which failed not to solace and ennoble the highest minds of ancient Greece and Rome— better claims than any of these? Is it beyond the bounds of possibility or of hope that the religion of rational piety, which was before Catholicism and is quite independent of it, may some day take its place,— a religion free from dogmas, and based solely on pure monotheism and on that belief or hope of immortality which we have seen to have been so real and general in the old pre-Christian world?

Happily it is in this direction that Protestant Christianity has long been tending. The intellectual breach between Protestants and Catholics has widened into an abyss. Their divergence touches no longer merely the details but the very fundamentals of belief. From orthodox Catholicism most Protestants are as far removed as they are from Confucianism; all recognising, at least in theory, the claims of reason, and only differing in the degree to which they use it. But the gulf is scarcely less wide between the Protestants of to-day and the Protestants of the Reformation. Many of us, Protestants though we are, have no more in common with the theology of Luther or of Latimer than with that of St. Augustine or St. Simeon Stylites. Stronger religious affinities connect us with Seneca or Porphyry than with any of the early Christian theologians; and, to put the matter truthfully, our rationalised Christianity is simply the higher philosophy of Paganism, with a different phraseology of course, but the same in substance with that which was taught and preached in the Roman Empire by Stoic, Platonist, and Pythagorean, in the days before the fanatics, who miscalled themselves Christians, drowned the sound reason of the world in the torrent of their all-overwhelming ignorance. The name of Christian is our only point of union with the primitive or with the reformed Church; nor is there any reason why the old name should cease to be borne, when it shall be openly and honestly avowed that the only sense in which it is used, outside the pale of Rome, is as a word significative of a mode or spirit of life, not of assent to certain articles of belief, formulated by Councils of unphilosophical theologians, who quarrelled about everything that was immaterial and settled nothing that was intelligible. The Christianity of the coming time need be none the less true and real for its frank admission of the fact that, as hitherto used in history, the word has been misapplied and misappropriated, having been the appellation of men whom historical records prove to have failed as signally in acting up to the Christian standard as in appreciating or comprehending its meaning. And thus, while in one sense the world may seem to grow less Christian, in another and better sense it may become more so; for the further we place ourselves from Christianity as revealed in history, the nearer shall we approximate in spirit to Christianity as originally propounded. In this way Christianity and Philosophy, which need never have been divided, may come, to the great benefit of the world, to be reunited and reconciled.

APPENDIX

As some aid to the memory of the chief religious and moral ideas contained in the works of the principal Pagan writers in the first ages of Christianity, I have done my best to reproduce them in the following verses. It is only necessary to say that I have hardly used a phrase, and certainly not a sentiment, that is not to be found in the original works. It is better of course to read the authors themselves, either in the originals or in the admirable translations which exist of them, and I only pretend to minister in this respect to those who have not the leisure that admits of a more extensive study of these great authors. As regards Epicurus, my authority is almost entirely the quotations from him or the references to him scattered through the works of Seneca. The terms "God" and "the gods" are used throughout as synonymous, as in the originals.

EPICTETUS

This problem first and most perplexes man,
Is there a God? or hath His rule a plan?
For some His Being, some His love deny,
Deeming His action bounded by the sky.

But who can doubt of God's good Providence,
Who blinds not to its proofs his every sense ?
Who made the eye made things for it to see ;
What need, without it, for such things to be ?
And if the parts of objects made by man
Reveal their maker's purpose and his plan,
How shall not Nature point to His design
Who made not sight without the sun to shine ?
Take lesser things : Who made it come to pass
That wool should come from skins, or milk from grass ?
Who made so many things together fit
With greater art than ever chance could hit ?
Thou durst say, No one ! Shameless that thou art
To use thy reason in so poor a part !

See man alone endowed with power of mind ;
See brutes without it for his use designed,
Fulfilling these, as food or tools, their end,
Whilst ours is God's great works to apprehend.

What should we then, but one and all upraise
From grateful hearts to God glad hymns of praise ?
And if all others fail to bless His name,
There shall be one who will, though old and lame ;
I for all others will the greatness sing
Of God, our common Father, Saviour, King,
Deeming so spent my human reason best
And so persisting till He bids me rest.

Round all His sons rests God's paternal care,
To each imparted for his guardian here
Part of Himself, small fraction of the whole,
Call it thy reason, conscience, or thy soul.

Be then in all things mindful of thy birth,
Offspring of Heaven, no mere child of earth.
A God thou bearest, not of man's device,
Mere gold or silver, bought at trifling price,
But Zeus Himself; Him darest thou pollute
By shameful thoughts or actions dissolute?
Shall that pure reason, intellect Divine,
Not all things see who made the sun to shine?
Shall thy closed doors ensure thee solitude,
Or darkened room thine infamies seclude?
God and thy conscience will be there with thee,
Needing no light thine acts or thoughts to see.
If God's mere image would thy guilt restrain,
Shall His all-seeing presence prove more vain?
Wilt thou His noblest workmanship debase,
And live to His as well as thy disgrace?
Wilt thou whom He made thine own guardian here,
And bade keep free from passion, lust, and fear,
False to thy nature and thy trust no less,
Prove by thy life thine own unworthiness?

An all-providing Deity confessed,
Who sees thine every thought, thine inmost breast,
To imitate, so far as mortal can,
His sublime virtues thy clear task as man.
Make His perfections thine unceasing aim;
Is God beneficent? Be thou the same.
Is He magnanimous, pure, faithful, free?
Be the same attributes displayed by thee.

As well, where robbers haunt the road, essay
To pass unaided, as on life's rough way,

Without a friend in whom thou durst confide
Against the foes who lurk on every side.
So seek a faithful comrade for thy life,
To guide thee safely through its storm and strife;
Yet trust not Man, frail as thyself at best,
Cæsar himself as mortal as the rest.
Trust God; attach thyself to Him alone;
"How?" By conforming to His will thine own.
"Have I a fever?" 'Tis God's will—and mine,—
My will a reflex of the will Divine,
His wish my wish, e'en though it be to die,
Or under torture on the rack to lie;
Only my body have men power to kill,
Not Zeus Himself can dominate my will.

Nature produced thee noble, modest, free,
Wouldst thou be happy, follow her decree;
Thy weal or woe she placed in thy control.
When she made both dependent on thy soul;
Value that higher than all else besides
Wherein alone true happiness resides;
Set not thy greatest good, thy greatest ill,
In aught that lies external to thy will;
Rank, riches, health, may flee thee in an hour,
Virtue alone rests always in thy power.

How wide thy duties! thy domain how great!
All men thy brothers, and the world thy state!
For all are parts of one connected whole
Who from one Father share His reasoning soul.
As member then of that great brotherhood,
Before thy private seek the general good.

As son or brother, whatsoe'er thou art,
Act in each station as becomes thy part;
Thy very slave treat gently, as divine;
God is his Father, who is also thine.

Let this thought help thee bear thy wrongs on earth,
Error, not malice, gives injustice birth.
Men err from imperfection of the will,
Mistaking ill for good or good for ill;
The bad need pity like the deaf or blind—
No blackness like the blackness of the mind.
Let not then fruitless anger fill thy breast,
Forgiveness, not revenge, becomes thee best.
For thou art human, born no savage brute;
Does Nature bid thee kick, bite, execute?
Nay, but to aid and benefit thy kind,
Endowed for this with sympathetic mind.

Nor seek from virtuous action further gain
Than to have done a just act or humane;
Who at Olympia his strength essays
Seeks no reward beyond the victor's bays,
But thou must combat in a sterner strife,
The real Olympian contest is with life;
No grander combat, no sublimer goal
Than for the sovereign freedom of thy soul.
As sailors to the Dioscuri kneel
When raging tempests toss their fragile keel,
So call on God thy saving aid to be,
Who only can be, through life's stormier sea,
Where false appearances the soul assail,
And fiercest passions blow a fiercer gale.

If such God's laws, obey them, or expect
The penalties assigned to their neglect;
No greater (yet what greater could there be?)
Than to fall short of man's humanity.

Life's but a voyage; I choose the ship, the crew,
Come storm, come wreck, what more have I to do?
Fearless to drown, with no blaspheming cry,
Knowing myself a mortal, born to die.
To me to throw the dice; to fate the rest;
My part to use the numbers for the best.
My prayer but this: that death find me intent
On some great work, humane, benevolent,
Or on mine own soul's culture, so that I
Stretching my dying hands to God may cry:
"Well have I used the powers I had from Thee,
Thine was my life, all things Thy gift to me,
Freely I render, grateful for their loan,
To Thy disposal what was ne'er mine own,
In this rejoicing, that no act of mine
Has once disgraced Thy government Divine,
That never thought of mine at Thy decree
Has murmured blame at what was sent from Thee."

Mortal, esteem thyself not meanly blest
With sight and reason to have been the guest
At God's great festival of life and light,
A brief spectator of that glorious sight.
Admire, applaud, but when the feast is o'er,
Depart adoring, not demanding more;
Make place for other claimants to their right
To all once ministrant to thy delight.

Resist not God, His signal prompt obey,
Wife, children, goods, He gave who takes away;
All from the first belonged to Him alone;
Thou losest nothing who hast naught thine own.

These are the terms of entrance to life's show;
Should they displease thee, thou art free to go;
For He who bade thee bade no grumbling guest;
A glad spectator pleases Him the best.

It best behoves thee tarry here below
Till God the signal gives that bids thee go;
At longest, short the time thou must remain,
At greatest, small *thy* share of human pain.
But, come the worst, wide open stands the door,
Go, cease to suffer; or, complain no more.
As little children, tired, desist from play,
No moment longer than thou choosest stay.
If only slightly smokes thy room, submit,
If beyond bearing thou art free to quit;
God in His mercy left the egress wide;
Only with reason, not in haste, decide.

When God recalls thee, go, nor be dismayed,
For only gods the universe pervade;
No Styx nor flames of Hell await thee there,
Who but returnest whence thou camest here;
Thy body dead and given back to earth
Rejoins the elements that gave it birth;
Thy soul, dissevered from its earthly chains,
To Soul returning, its real home regains;
Death, the last refuge, ultimate release,
For all the portal of eternal peace.

MARCUS AURELIUS

I

One doom, the same, for all on earth,
    Oblivion for evermore!
    In endless time behind, before,
Thy task to make thy life of worth.

All things are borne time's stream adown
    Too swiftly overmuch to prize;
    As well desire yon bird that flies,
And is no sooner seen than flown.

Across the desert's changeless face
    The drifting sands still look the same;
    Men follow men, yet all their fame
Is constant only to their race.

Springs come and go, and from the trees
    The fresh green leaves soon sere and fall;
    Like leaves we pass, and leaves are all
Who cast their praises on the breeze,

Who hold the keys of shame or fame,
    Frail vessels, doomed themselves to die,
    To whom we trust our memory,
And just the knowledge of our name.

Then what remains? This, this alone:
    To bless the gods with reverent soul,
    And, with broad tolerant self-control,
To make the good of all thine own;

To live in word and thought sincere;
To friends, to slaves, to kinsmen kind;
Thy soul at peace, thine heart resigned
To all that God hath ordered here.

II

Know; Zeus, the Greatest and the Best,
A portion of His glorious mind
Hath lent to guard and guide mankind,
A god to dwell within thy breast.

Philosophy but teaches this:
To reverence that God within,
To keep that Reason pure from sin,
In godlike calm and godlike bliss.

He fights the noblest fight, he prays
Best to the gods who, passionless,
Untouched by pleasure or distress,
Preserves his reason all his days;

Whose soul admits no thought of shame;
Who hopes no good, who fears no ill
From aught beyond his power or will,
From life, death, health, wealth, want, or fame;

Who makes his soul retreat more sure
Than are for others hills or seas,
Nor seeks from trouble gentler ease
Than flows from tranquil thoughts and pure.

III

That pleases me which pleases Thee,
   Great Universe; I murmur not,
   But deem the evils of my lot
Part of the world's grand harmony.

This is to follow God—to bend
   Freely and gladly to His will,
   Without complaint, and trustful still,
Though all thine hopes in grief should end.

The gods must rule things for the best,
   Or if—the evil thought be hence—
   There are no gods, nor Providence,
And praise and prayer rise all unblest,

Still to thy Nature be thou true;
   Rome is thy State as Antonine,
   But, as a man, the world is thine,
That larger State demands thee too.

Thy Nature teaches: Live for others;
   Like branches on the self-same tree
   Men form but one community;
Love thy compatriots and brothers.

Their good in all thine acts pursue;
   Live every day as if thy last;
   Thy conduct, till life's warfare's past,
Calm, kind, contented, just, and true.

IV

The gods, with loving, untired mind,
   Long ages through, men's faults forgive;
   Thou, with thy few short years to live,
Learn to be patient of thy kind.

Should men injure or revile thee,
   Requite with love their hatred still;
   Show them they know not good from ill;
Think not they wrong thee wittingly.

Thy soul, thy self, is made no worse,
   For all the malice men may show,
   Than is the crystal fountain's flow
Polluted by some careless curse.

Who wrongs thee, does himself the wrong;
   Forgiveness is the nobler part;
   Passion betrays the wounded heart,
Wrath proves thee weak, as mercy strong.

Let this thought, too, for others plead,
   To bear their wrongs with gentleness:
   That thou, like them, dost oft transgress,
That thine own failings pardon need.

V

So live thine hour; nor count it loss
   To go to dwell with gods above,
   Or—if there be no gods that love—
To leave a world of Chance and Force.

Thy life-voyage ended, disembark,
  And either wake to happier life,
  Or, freed for ever from the strife,
Be thankful for the restful dark.

Death is a passage or a close;
  Each stage of life is bridged by death,
  Each moment's giving of the breath
Prepares thee for thy last repose.

What were a few years more or less?
  The players change; their parts are old;
  The play a thousand times retold
Were naught but grief and weariness.

What has been, is; what is, will be;
  Things circle in a changeless groove;
  Ten thousand years in forty move;
To-day contains eternity.

To each his hour. All future time
  Will bring to bloom no lovelier rose
  Than this spring in thy garden blows;
No fruit more splendid at its prime.

Change is life's law, and death the last;
  Nor gods nor Nature wish thee ill;
  Where is no fault of heart or will,
No shame upon the soul is cast.

So wait, with patient willing heart,
  (Thy life-post held, thy duty done),
  The signal of thy warfare won,
The final summons to depart;

And then, with grateful sweet content,
As the ripe olive falls to earth
Blessing the tree which gave it birth,
To Nature render what she lent.

SENECA

If, with our reason we attempt to scan
Of this great world the fundamental plan,
We reach at last one all-pervading Soul—
God, who created and preserves the whole,
First Cause of causes. Call Him as we will,
Fate, Chance, or Providence proclaim Him still;
His presence fills His whole creation's frame,
And God and Nature differ but in name;
The myriad phases of His single might
The gods but show in number infinite;
Though Jove or Bacchus serve Him for a name,
Under a thousand names He rests the same.

Who rightly know God, worship Him the best,
His power no greater than His love confessed;
No need to raise to Heaven thine hands in prayer,
Or vex with foolish vows an idol's ear,
God is close to thee, ever at thy side,
With thee, within thee, witness, guardian, guide;
Naught it avails to hide thyself from men,
No thought nor act is hidden from His ken.
He needs no temples reared aloft of stone,
Who in each hallowed heart prefers His throne;
He asks no reeking victims at thine hand;
A soul pure, upright, is His sole demand.

We do God wrong to fear Him; love alone
Is due to Him by whom but love is shown.
The gods are good, the source of nothing ill,
Nor could they injure, even with the will;
Man from the first has been their constant care,
Their aim his welfare, and their guide his prayer:
'Tis not their anger shakes the earth, nor tears
The skies with tempests or men's hearts with fears.

If God thus rules, how comes it, some complain,
The good are not exempt from grief and pain,
But suffer countless variants of woe
Which oft the wicked neither feel nor know?
Enlarge thy vision, and this truth thou'lt see,
Wretched they may be called, but cannot be;
From all real evils God protects them still
Who count no evils real but those of will.
The good as special objects of His love
God fits by trial for their life above,
The more the ills wherewith they have to strive,
The more the force wherewith their virtues thrive;
Nor less the salt sea changes for the rain
Than they from evil feel or take the stain.

The gods give life, Philosophy gives more,
Teaching to live that life by virtue's law.
Wouldst thou from all man's greater ills live free,
Give thyself wholly to Philosophy;
Thy soul to all, by God ordained, resigned,
Thy conduct ruled by love for all mankind.
Make, like the gods, beneficence thine end,
Freely for others thy best powers expend;

The want or burthen under which they groan
At thine own cost and labour make thine own.
Nor let thy native country bound thy zeal,
But deem the world itself thy commonweal;
Let thy forbearance no exception know,
Nor grudge the asked-for mercy to thy foe;
Shelter the exile, liberate the slave,
Here from misfortune, there from hunger save.
Though man, ungrateful, doubts the gods' goodwill,
True to their nature they shed blessings still;—
Despite of all thy gifts bestowed in vain,
Like them, unwearied, freely give again.

Count all men equal, fellow-slaves of fate,
One common bondage holds us, small or great;
Nobles or slaves all have one origin,
One common Father makes us all akin;
And all alike, or high or low our birth,
One common Virtue makes of equal worth.
Man's mind, not birth, determines his degree;
No slave so mean but virtue sets him free.
What if his body's bound! His soul can rise
On wings of thought unfettered to the skies.
What if his body's bought! His soul is free;
No servitude can mar its liberty.
Deem that not held by local bounds of space
Which has the universe for dwelling-place;
Nor bound by time, which has the power to see
Through ages past and ages yet to be.

Nature made Virtue man's chief aim and goal
When she made Conscience mistress of his soul,

For all our good deeds no more grateful praise
Than that which conscience to itself conveys;
No penalty for crime we have to fear
Worse than an injured conscience makes us bear.
Virtue calls all, and easy of access,
Spreads smooth the road that leads to happiness;
Mountains may crumble, Etna fall away,
True virtue only suffers no decay,
But, like the stars, bright with eternal light,
Still guards the same unalterable height,
Whereon as harmless as on seas the rain
Falls with full force misfortune, grief, or pain.
It takes no increase from reward or praise,
Nor weighs felicity by length of days,
But from the moments of each act sublime
Enjoys the fulness of eternal time.

For good, not long, life is the wise man's prayer;
Not when, but how, he dies, his only care.
Too high the price at which life may be bought;
He lives not whilst he can, but whilst he ought,
Holding it true, that each man rightly dies
Who thus from danger to right living flies.
To live in no one's power—to man alone
God gave by placing death within his own,
With this great solace softening every ill,
That no man's held to life against his will.
Should o'er thy reason ceaseless pain prevail,
Or cureless malady thy strength assail,
Should age take from thee all of life but breath,
What nearer refuge couldst thou wish than death?

Nor few the roads that lead to liberty—
Yon precipice, well, river, or the sea;
From all incurable disease or pain
An easy outlet flows through every vein.
Yet shouldst thou still, for love of friend or wife,
Bear to its end at worst the load of life;
No greater proof of love that thou canst give
Than for another to consent to live.

But of the evils which we suffer here
The worst are those our follies make us bear.
What greater madness than for no just cause
To rush to senseless sanguinary wars,
And at a price for peace itself too dear
Ten thousand evils to inflict and bear?
If wild beasts kill, 'tis not without a cause,
Hunger or vengeance whets their teeth and claws;
But man alone, endowed with gentler mind,
Joys in the causeless bloodshed of his kind.
No bounds our cruel avarice heeds or knows,
For lust of gain we make the world our foes;
Deeds which as crimes are branded by the law
Whole senates sanction or command in war,
And murders foul for which the felon dies
Done by the soldier all applaud and prize.

Death has no after terrors for the wise;
No flaming rivers haunt his closing eyes;
For him mere fables all that poets tell
Of future judgments, or of pains in Hell;
For him the faith, that death or ends all woes
Or leads to life exempt from grief or close.

Of these two ends (no third or worse in view)
'Tis fair and best to hope the brighter true :
That life's a prelude to a happier state,
Where brighter destinies thy soul await.
The day thou fearest as thy last on earth,
Of life immortal is the day of birth.
Then shall thy soul, freed from the body's chain,
Its birthplace, Heaven, purified regain,
Finding no strangeness in that boundless air,
Where first it sojourned ere it sojourned here ;
There shall thy mind in greater light, not less,
Trace Nature's secrets to their last recess,
Learn the great mystery of that wondrous force
Which set the stars, and keeps them, in their course
And mindful still of those whom late it fled,
Hold commune with the spirits of the dead.

So count the dead not lost for evermore ;
They have not left us, only gone before.
The death that severs, does not end, our love,
Who are but pilgrims to a home above,
Where, reunited, neither hill nor plain,
Distance nor discord, shall divide again.

Nor mourn the shortness of the life of man ;
The world itself endures but for a span.
Not man alone declines from stage to stage ;
The very stars advance from youth to age ;
The time may differ, but the law is one
Which kills a mortal or puts out a sun.
Nor hold for perished any life that's closed ;
Nothing is ended, only decomposed.

Things pass from life to life, and nothing dies
But life itself to some fresh form supplies.
So, too, when God, destroying every trace
That ever proved the presence of our race,
By flame or flood, shall once again disperse
Back to its elements this universe,
Another world shall from that ruin rise,
And other stars shed splendour from the skies,
Then shall another race their course begin,
Blameless of crime and innocent of sin,
And all things else shall come again to birth
To glory in a renovated earth.

EPICURUS

Wouldst thou as man live truly free?
   Then, setting store by naught beside
   Of all that claims to aid or guide,
Serve as a slave Philosophy.

To these two things alone thy prayer
   Of all men covet be confined:
   A body free from pain; a mind
Unruffled by desire or care.

Avoid to mingle in the strife
   That rages round the helm of State,
   But, undisturbed by praise or hate,
Live out the nobler hidden life.

Pleasure is all men's aim and goal;
  They find it most who seek it least,
  Less in the riot or the feast
Than in contentment of the soul.

Happy his life who asks but this;
  No fortune can his peace destroy,
  Loud shall he still proclaim his joy
Though in the bull of Phalaris.

Full rich is he who seeks no more
  Than Nature to his need supplies;
  He who, with much, for more still sighs,
Though master of the world is poor;

And many they who live to find,
  In riches heaped up year by year,
  Changed, but not ended, all their care,
And new the trouble of their mind.

They badly live who life begin
  With each fresh hope that Chance inspires,
  And with ne'er-satisfied desires
Count nothing won, but all to win.

For few there be who come to die
  But part from life as just begun,
  Counting their course as still to run,
Regardless of the years that fly.

Nor wise are they who trembling view
  The chances of the days to be,
  And like the ever-changing sea,
Each day begin their lives anew.

But greater folly still is theirs
    Who, tired of life, cut short its thread,
    If to this consequence has led
Mere misuse of the passing years.

Be thou more grateful for thy past;
    Count all wherewith thou hast been blest
    Though past, not gone, but still possessed,
Thy best possession to the last;

And, to live well thy span of days,
    Hold some good man in memory,
    And deeming him still watching thee,
His blame eschew, deserve his praise.

When round thee throngs the multitude
    With pressure of its speech and law,
    Then chiefly in thyself withdraw
And in thy soul seek solitude.

Leave to the crowd its faiths, its fears,
    Its dread of angry gods on high;
    The gods in calm passivity
Care naught for praises nor for prayers.

Leave to the crowd its fears of death,
    Or terrors that beyond may lie;
    The worst can come to all who die
Is but cessation of the breath.

Who thus will his desires confine
    To healthful sense and fearless soul,
    Holds happiness in his control
And leads as man the life divine.

PLUTARCH ON SUPERSTITION

Few of the ills we mortals bear
Excel or equal those we fear;
But worst his lot of all mankind
Whom superstitious terrors bind.
He dreads no storm who stays on shore,
Nor battle, who goes not to war;
But he who thinks of God with dread
Has terror always overhead,
And draws one long unending fear
Alike from land, and sea, and air.
For him no respite nor release,
For him in sleep itself no peace,—
Sleep from which even felons gain
A moment's respite from their pain;—
New torments each fresh night supplies
New fears from each last dream arise.

A slave may always hope to find
A master of a gentler mind;
But he who fears the gods above,
Who reads malevolence for love,
Who dreads that Power to whom we owe
The countless blessings here we know,
And for whose aid in prayer we plead
To excellence in thought and deed,
That man, fly wheresoe'er he will,
His tyranny shall hold him still.

Death to his misery sets no end
Whose fears beyond this life extend,

Who after all life's ills are past
Dreads never-ending ones at last;
In Hell before him yawning wide
Sees all known pains intensified,
Shudders at streams of liquid fire,
Grim spectres, judges, tortures dire,—
From such vain fancies suffering more
Than ever from real ills he bore.

Not such the atheist, whose mind
To all Divinity is blind;
Blind where it least becomes to be,
Blind where it most concerns to see,
Not knowing aught of God above,
Who rules us with a Father's love.
For him exist no powers divine;
No need to heed them, if benign;
Beneath misfortune's rude assault
At least he holds no gods at fault,
But frets at worst at Chance or Fate,
Whose blows he yet may palliate,
Nor looks, for all he may endure,
Beyond himself for cause or cure.

But he who deems no chance so slight
But Providence had him in sight,
Who, if his body somewhat ails,
Or children die, or fortune fails,
Of sinners cries himself the worst,
Of God and angels both accursed,
Accepts his malady or grief
As penalty beyond relief,

In sackcloth courts the public gaze,
Rolls prostrate, sacrifices, prays,
If haply so he may atone
For the great sin that makes him groan,
In that he tasted such a meat,
Or found perchance such wine too sweet;—
What can one such a man proclaim
But atheist in all but name?
For God exists against his will
Who charges Him with every ill,
And fear, not love, inspires his prayer
Who fain would doubt could he but dare.

If irreligion thrives on earth,
'Twas superstition gave it birth;
No faults in Nature led mankind
To doubt in God, whose ruling mind
First gave and still supplies the force
That moves the stars in ordered course,
That through fixed seasons draws the year
Turns day to night, makes trees to bear;
No imperfections here gave rise
To disbelief and dark surmise,
No, 'twas the foolishness of priests,
The services of slaughtered beasts,
The long procession wending slow
Round altars with dull chants of woe,
The senseless charm, the magic prayer,
The penances of sinful fear,
The body smeared with mud, to show
The whiteness of the soul below;—

These were the things that made men say
Better no gods to whom to pray
Than gods like those to whom the crowd
In this vile servitude is bowed;
Gods of no higher nobler worth
Than their mean worshippers on earth.

Were it not better if the Gaul
Believed there were no gods at all
Than in his terror feigned them such
That naught but human blood can touch
Their hearts with pity, or assuage
The fire of their remorseless rage?
Or what of that worst scene of vice,
The Carthaginian sacrifice,
When round the image of the god
The pious crowd exultant trod,
And mothers gave, nor thought it shame,
Their little ones to feed the flame
In Saturn's honour, whilst the sound
Of hymn, and prayer, and music drowned
The feeble unavailing cry
Of infants doomed for God to die?
Ah! better had they never heard
The name of God than thus been stirred
To make the glory of His name
The pretext for their deeds of shame!

The sage, who thought the sun to be
A stone, was charged with blasphemy,
But none would the Cimmerians blame
For calling it an empty name;

And so, methinks, they wrong God less
Who doubt or disbelief confess
Than they who worse of God believe
Than of a man they could conceive,
And every vice to Him assign
To prove Him fickle, false, malign;
As I would rather men should say
"There is no Plutarch" than that they
Should speak of Plutarch as so mean,
So full of petty spite and spleen,
That, if you vexed him in the least,
Into your crops he'd turn his beast.

From superstition then to flee
Should he resolve who would live free,
And shunning piety's excess
To shun its contrary no less,
Careful to hold that golden mean
Which lies the two extremes between,
Not negligent of Him whose care
Is round us always everywhere,
Nor serving Him like slaves, whose zeal
But indicates the fear they feel;
But worshipping with pious trust
The All-beneficent and Just,—
Love the sole tribute to be paid
For all the love to us displayed.

www.ingramcontent.com/pod-product-compliance
Lightning Source LLC
Chambersburg PA
CBHW031951230426
43672CB00010B/2119